The Bell Ringer

The Bell Ringer

Victor Rodriguez

THE
WATERCRESS
PRESS

San Antonio

2005

A Watercress Press book
from *Geron & Associates*

Cover and book design by Fishead Productions

For additional copies,
order from The Twig Bookstore,
5005 Broadway, San Antonio, TX 78209
1-800-729-8944
email: twig@thetwig.com

ISBN # 0-934955-63-8
Library of Congress Catalog Card Number 2005934884

Introduction

The writing of this book is an attempt to preserve some personal experiences and to give at least token recognition to some individuals who so unselfishly helped to shape my world. These individuals were proud people who had the courage to stand by their personal convictions during a period when conformity to popular practice or belief might have been the easier route to follow.

And of equal importance, this is also an attempt to preserve the memory of Manuela, our mother, who gave us each day a renewed feeling of hope for a better tomorrow. As she blew out the old kerosene lamp every night, you would hear her say, *"Hasta mañana con el favor de Dios"* – "Until tomorrow, with God's favor."

Sometimes when I was less than enthusiastic about getting up early to ring the church bell, she would encourage me by reminding me that I had been hand-picked to perform this task by Lucille Lindberg, my teacher. "I'm proud of you," she would say in her quiet reassuring tone, and then she would add, "Being a bell ringer is a responsibility that will teach you many things that will benefit you for the rest of your life."

Victor Rodriguez

September 29, 2005
San Antonio, Texas

Contents

Part III — San Antonio, 1957 —

Illustrations

PART I
GROWING UP IN SOUTH TEXAS
1932-1951

Returning Home

Victor Rodriguez was born on February 27, 1932, in the small ranching and farming community of Inez near the Gulf Coast in South Texas. His father, Augustine Rodriguez, was a tenant farmer who lived off the land. Victor had four sisters, three older and one younger. His father was illiterate and placed very little value on education; this was the Depression era, and he was concerned with survival, not education. But Victor's mother Manuela insisted that her daughters attend school and they did, much to the dismay of Augustine who felt that a woman's place was in the home.

When Victor was four years old, his father died, and Manuela was left with the entire responsibility of raising and supporting the family. Victor's oldest sister was ten and the youngest only three. Since Manuela could not continue as a tenant farmer, she decided that the family should move to Edna, a small town nine miles from Inez.

Edna is a hundred miles west of Houston, and Corpus Christi is seventy miles farther south. The main occupations here were ranching and farming. Of the population of 5500, about 55 percent were Anglo-Americans; of the rest, Mexican-Americans constituted about 30 percent and African-Americans were the remaining 15 percent.

For the most part, the English-speaking people of Edna were good, honest, hard-working and law-abiding citizens. Prior to the early 1950s their general attitude toward Mexican-Americans was consistent with the contemporary view of most Anglos throughout Southwest Texas. The Mexican-Americans were segregated in a school which consisted of grades one through four. They were not permitted to be served in the eating establishments.

It was under these circumstances that Victor's mother managed to raise her family in Edna. The children played, worked, were educated, and grew up there. Although none of them live there today, they still proudly refer to Edna as "our hometown."

Manuela Rodriguez

Victor left Edna in 1951 to attend college on an athletic scholarship. In the succeeding fifty years, he graduated from a university, served two years in the Army, and worked thirty-six years with the San Antonio School District until his retirement in 1994. In the spring of 2000, he went back to Edna to attend the 49th reunion of the class of 1951.

* * *

The car trip from San Antonio to Edna took a little over two hours. During the drive, Victor's wife, Flo, sat quietly next to him enjoying the view of fields covered with thousands of wild flowers. During the past fifty years Victor had returned to Edna on a few occasions but most of his visits had been brief. One of his longest stays had been just a year ago. The school board had fired the superintendent of schools and Victor was among half a dozen individuals who were interviewed for the position of interim superintendent. The board voted unanimously to hire Victor until they could find a permanent superintendent. It had been a short stay, with no time to renew old friendships. Now he was hoping to see his classmates, some of whom he had not seen since graduation night.

Approaching the bridge which spans the Navidad River on the outskirts of Edna on Highway 59, it seemed to him that the old bridge was different. Somehow, it did not appear as impressive to him as it had during his younger days. It seemed to be narrower and shorter. Victor had spent the summer after high school graduation working for the Texas Highway Department on the widening of this bridge.

4

The old bridge held other memories for him as well. The Navidad River which flowed lazily beneath it had provided the main source of recreation during the hot summer months. It was here that the boys had learned to swim. He wondered what had happened to those swimmers — Jesse Gonzales, Albert Farias, Edward Nava, Andrew Garza, Louis Barrera . . . Most of them had dropped out of school at the end of the fourth grade. He wondered if any of them were still here in Edna. Were they married? How many children did they have now? Had any of them left for a better opportunity elsewhere? And then the big question crossed his mind: How far could they go and how much of an opportunity would they find with only a fourth-grade education? Victor looked down at the river as they neared the far end of the bridge. The water looked a little dirty to him now, but forty-nine years ago they had walked over four miles to swim and play there.

As they entered the city limits of Edna, he slowed the car a little, beginning to recognize some of the old landmarks and places that had been a part of his environment as a child and a teenager. On the edge of town he saw where Frank Herrera's place used to be on the left side of the highway. This had once been a dance hall but Frank converted it into a saloon and pool hall.

In the center of town he stopped at a traffic light, and he saw many people walking, but none of their faces were familiar. Forty-nine years now seemed like a long time. The old courthouse had been torn down and in its place stood a modern air-conditioned facility. He wondered how many Mexican-American lawyers had practiced in this new facility. Gus Garcia, a lawyer from San Antonio, had set the precedent in the old court-house in 1952 when he became the first Mexican-American lawyer to defend a client there in the now famous Pedro Hernandez case.

Gus Garcia appealed the murder conviction of Hernandez, a migrant cottonpicker Victor had met in the cotton fields around Edna. Hernandez was convicted for the shooting death of Joe Espinosa in an Edna bar next to the Mexican barbershop where Victor was getting a haircut at the time of the shooting. Garcia and his law partner went before the Federal Supreme Court in 1954 and argued that Hispanics were a separate class in this community and were not treated equally by the courts. Four months later, Chief Justice Earl Warren rendered the unanimous opinion declaring that people could not be excluded from jury duty because of national origin. As a result, Hernandez was retried. He was again found guilty and received a life sentence, but this marked the beginning for Hispanics to serve on juries in Edna and many other Texas courts where they had previously been excluded.

The traffic light turned green and Victor continued driving slowly into the heart of town. He saw that some of the businesses and restaurants had undergone changes, at least from their outward appearance. But he remembered the way things used to be. He remembered when a Mexican-American could not be served in a restaurant's main dining room but was required to go around to the back door to order a hamburger or a sandwich to go. He remembered Mexican-Americans kidding each other about the fact that there were no doorbells on the back doors. They made the best of a bad situation by poking fun at each other. They even had their own criteria for evaluating the cooks and determining whether they were "good cooks" or "bad cooks." This had little to do with how good or bad the food tasted. Some of the cooks were rude and disliked waiting on them when they knocked on the back doors of their kitchens. Sometimes they would make them wait twenty or thirty minutes before they acknowledged the knocking, and when they did condescend to take the order, they would give them food that was poorly prepared and charge them a little more than the normal cost. Victor and his friends suspected they were pocketing the extra change. These were the ones they labeled "bad cooks."

The "good cooks," as they called them, were sympathetic. They took the back-door orders promptly and most of the time they gave an extra portion of whatever was ordered. As soon as the cook handed them their order, they would make a statement such as "one hamburger to go." The words "to go" meant that the boss of the cafe was near so they would take their order and leave so as not to create any problem for the cook.

He recalled some of the pranks they played when he and his friends were 14 or 15. The fact that they were not allowed to eat in these restaurants was a source of personal embarrassment to them. Once in a while, a Mexican-American from out of town would stop in Edna and look for a place to eat. The local boys played a game with these out-of-town Mexican-Americans when they asked about a "good" place to eat. If they liked them they would explain the local situation and direct them to the doors where the "good cooks" worked. But if they didn't like them, they gave the name of a restaurant where they knew Mexican-Americans would not be served. They would tell them how clean the place was and how friendly the owner was. They even told them about the good food that was reasonably priced and about the good-looking waitresses who worked there.

When the out-of-towners entered the front door of the recommended establishments, Victor and his friends took turns peeking through the windows to see how the out-of-towner fared. If there were five or six in their group, they would get up a pot to which each contributed a nickel. The object of the game was to see which one could most accurately predict how long the out-of-town Mexican-American could stay inside before he was asked to leave. The person who made the most accurate prediction won the pot. Their rules were rather rigid, too. The actual time was determined by the closing of the door behind the Mexican-American visitor when he entered the cafe and the closing of the door behind him when he left. Sometimes they stayed inside for one minute and sometimes as long as twenty minutes. It depended on how soon they had a confrontation with the owner or how long they would sit there and be ignored while everyone stared at them. Some would stay for ten or fifteen minutes before their curiosity got the best of them. Then they called a waitress and were shocked when told that Mexican-Americans were not allowed in this restaurant. On other occasions, the waitress would ignore their summons and go get the boss.

Victor wondered now how they could have been so cruel as to subject others to the same kind of humiliation they had experienced. Why had they done it? Did they think that an outsider might perhaps break down some of the barriers that confronted them? Did they really believe that an outsider might bring some relief and provide instant change? Were they using this approach as a kind of harassment against the Anglo-American? Or were they waiting for someone else to instigate some kind of action to remedy the situation? This attitude of "let someone else do it" was a characteristic of the Mexican-American in those days.

Victor drove slowly through the center of town, beginning to wonder where he and Flo were going to spend the night. He had a few friends in Edna, but he didn't want to impose on them with an impromptu visit. He decided to stop at a motel he had noticed on the way into town, so he turned the car around and started back in the direction from which they had come. He stopped in front of the motel's office, and while Flo waited in the car he went inside to ask if there were any vacancies. An elderly Anglo lady greeted him at the desk and he could feel her looking him over carefully. When he asked if she had a room for him and his wife she said yes and asked him to fill out the guest registration forms. When he finished the forms she glanced over them briefly and then her eyes returned to the registration card and she repeated his name slowly.

"Rodriguez . . . Rodriguez," she said. "Victor Rodriguez," she repeated and then asked, "Aren't you the Rodriguez boy whose mother was Manuela Rodriguez?"

"Yes," he replied, amazed that she remembered not only his mother's name, but she seemed to remember him as well.

She called out to her husband, who was in the back room. When an elderly man appeared in the doorway, she spoke to him in a loud voice and Victor assumed that he was hard of hearing.

"Do you know that this is Manuela's boy?" she asked him.

"Is that right?" replied the old man with a curious look and then he added, "I remember him. He's that Rodriguez boy who played football here some time back." Then, proving that he really remembered, he added, "He was a mighty fine track man, too." He turned to Victor. "I remember your mother very well."

"Yes," said the woman, "Manuela was a mighty fine woman."

"How long are you and your wife staying with us?" asked the old man. Victor told him they were just there for overnight. The motel manager and his wife both appeared disappointed, and the man added, "We're mighty pleased to see you again. You must be here for the 49-year reunion of the '51 class. Several of your friends are registered here, and I'll bet they'll be awfully glad to see you." He handed Victor a key and gave him directions to their room.

"If you need anything, just call us," said the woman. Victor thanked them and as he was walking out the door, he heard her say, "Manuela would be awfully proud."

He glanced at his watch and saw it was still mid-afternoon. The reunion was scheduled to start at 7:30 that evening.

Victor and Flo were tired from the trip and they decided to take a nap. Flo was exhausted and it didn't take her long to fall asleep, but Victor couldn't sleep so he lay there thinking about the amazing course his life had taken since he left Edna forty-nine years ago. He had worked hard during the years and had been blessed with one promotion after another. He had steadily climbed the ladder of success and six years ago he had retired as superintendent of the San Antonio Independent School District, the sixth largest school system in Texas.

As Victor's mind wandered back into the past, he was overcome by nostalgia. He lay there thinking about the old days that had been filled with a variety of experiences, some good and some bad, but all of which had made him wiser. . . .

Two Outstanding Teachers

Someone once said, "Your way of looking at the world determines what you see." The way one looks at the world is often affected by personal influences and experiences. Fortunate indeed are those of us who have survived our experiences with a true perspective of the world.

Edna was a most unusual community when Victor was growing up because it had three independent school districts within one. The Anglo schools were on the southeast side of town, the Black schools were on the east, and on the northwest side was a small, wood-framed building, about 35 by 40 feet, known as the Mexican-American school.

While Victor did not minimize the kind of formal education he received at the University of North Texas, Yale University, and, of course, that stellar flagship university of the Southwest, the University of Texas at Austin, still the best schooling he ever got was his first through the fourth grade years at the old Mexican-American school in the little town of Edna. And one of the very best teachers that he ever had was a lady named Lucille Lindberg.

The Mexican-American school contained four rows of desks, with ten desks in each row. There was one teacher. Lucille Lindberg was, in Victor's opinion, one of the truly outstanding individuals he met in his life. He benefitted from the instruction of Seymour Sarrison at Yale, Dr. L. D. Haskew at the University of Texas, and many others, and while he didn't belittle their contributions to his

Lucille Lindberg

formal education, he felt that the contributions of Lucille Lindberg at a rather difficult period of his life were the most significant, and they had served him well throughout the years.

* * *

It was on a Friday evening in 1936 when the Rodriguez family moved to Edna, and they arrived with all their personal belongings just as it was getting dark. The next morning, a blonde, blue-eyed, beautiful lady, about 5 feet 3, drove up in an old black Chevrolet. She got out on the muddy street, walked up the path, and knocked on the door of their house, which was a two-room shack.

"My name is Lucille Lindberg," she told Manuela, "and I am a teacher and I understand that you have some school-aged children." She convinced Manuela that her children should enroll in her school, even four-year-old Victor. She gave them directions to the school, about three miles away.

Manuela believed in education, and even though she could neither read nor write, she wanted her children to have a better opportunity than she had. So she agreed that she would send them to school on the following Monday.

To this day, it's still a mystery to Victor how a family could arrive on a Friday evening, and a teacher could know about it so fast. But Edna was a small town of 5,000 people. Miss Lindberg must have had a radar system to spot the Hispanics, because she knew they were there.

The Rodriguez children reported to school that Monday and she gave them each a set of rules. She said, "First-graders on row one, second-graders in row two," and so on. She had a kindergarten class when kindergarten was not even heard of in the United States, and she entertained the youngsters too young for school with toys in the back of the room. She even had some pre-kindergarten youngsters, and there was a free lunch program which she operated for the children who showed up with no food for lunch. The school had no running water, and there were two outdoor privies — one for the boys and one for the girls. (The boys' was a three-holer; the girls had a four-holer.) The school was located near a creek and when it rained the creek overflowed and the outdoor privies got a good washing out.

Besides reading, writing, and arithmetic, Lucille Lindberg also taught responsibility. She talked to the students about their civic responsibility and she gave each of them an assignment. On certain mornings, the entire school of forty Mexican-American children would pick up all the trash and debris on the schoolhouse lawn. That was their civic responsibility. When Victor reached the third grade, she assigned him to be the church-bell ringer for the Catholic Church. She said, "Father Smiers is looking for a church-bell ringer at St. Agnes," so Victor took on the job.

Miss Lindberg tried to teach some of the students to be artists, and she insisted that they all learn how to read — and she made no bones about it. Victor hated the thought of having to stand before the class to recite a poem, so when she gave him a thick book of poems by Robert Frost, he thumbed through it and picked the shortest one. It was called "The Fear of God." Victor thought because it had so few lines it was something he could memorize easily, but he soon discovered that it involved some pretty strenuous study because it was rather complex. Every time he stood before the class his knees began to shake, and he would start by saying, "The-e Fear of . . ." and then he would forget the rest of it and she would say, "God", and together they would get through it. And she would say, "Don't say 'Thee,' say 'Thuh.'" And so she taught them like this.

Victor and his sisters at a recent Rodriguez family gathering had laughed about the time when one of the sixteen-year-old fourth-graders tried to lock Miss Lindberg in a closet. She reacted by borrowing a knife from one of the boys (back then, anybody could carry a knife to school, and as a matter of fact, you weren't anybody if you didn't own a knife).

Then she went out to one of the huisache trees, cut off a pretty good switch, and knocked the thorns off of it (perhaps one or two thorns remained). She went back inside and proceeded to bend that sixteen-year-old over her desk and really give him some good licks. After that, they all looked upon Miss Lindberg with greatly increased respect.

But the students knew this: They knew that Lucille Lindberg truly, truly cared about them. They knew that she loved them. And every year, at the end of school, she would talk to the first-graders, second-graders, and third-graders and insist that they come back the following year. And to the fourth-graders she would say, "It's important that you continue your education. It's very important because this is America. And in America, if you work hard and are willing to compete, you can be anything that you want to be." She got no takers . . . that is, until Manuela Rodriguez listened to her.

Victor's paintings of his early morning runs with the dogs.

As Victor progressed through the third and fourth grades, he became famous as the bell ringer in Edna, because he not only woke the people up once in the morning, he woke them up twice. As he ran from where he lived in the old Black community, through town, through the Anglo neighborhood to the church, he woke up all the dogs. Every dog in town would start barking at him as he approached their territory. He soon learned a valuable lesson: In order to keep from being bitten he needed to stay in the middle of the road. He would trot down the middle of the road and every dog would make a run at him and then circle back. People would say, "What's going on? What's bothering Ol' Blue out there?" And someone else would answer, "Oh, it's nothing. That's just Manuela's boy running to ring the church bell."

The barking of the dogs at four-thirty in the morning woke up most of the people in their respective neighborhoods. Others were awakened at exactly five o'clock when, two miles away, the church bell started ringing. And then, after serving as an altar boy, Victor would run another mile to the Mexican-American school. There were no leash laws back in Edna, so it was every man and every dog for himself.

Victor ran barefoot and the soles of his feet were thicker than the soles on your shoes. Fortunately, the streets were made of sandy loam. He could outrun most of the dogs except for one named Adolph. This was a bulldog, and he was sneaky. He would hide behind a trash can, in a ditch, a culvert, or behind a tree, and since he couldn't run very fast because of his low center of gravity, he would sneak up on Victor. Besides Adolph the Bulldog, there was a golden retriever that Victor called Red, and a German shepherd named Fritz. But Victor survived those dogs, and all of them contributed to his future track career.

Lucille Lindberg convinced Victor's mother to continue the education of her children beyond the fourth grade, and as his sisters completed their four years in the Mexican-American school, Manuela would enroll them in the Anglo-American school. In the fall of 1942, at the end of his fourth-grade year, she enrolled him in the Anglo-American school. However, Victor and his sisters had to repeat the fourth grade in the new school because it was the general consensus in those days that the Mexican-American school provided a much lower level of education than the Anglo schools. One can imagine the surprise and shock of the fourth-grade teachers as they discovered that the Rodriguez children could read, write, and compute better than the other fourth-graders.

Victor and his sisters, Patricia, Rafaela, Theresa, Adela

And so Victor and his sisters continued their education, although they were not entirely accepted at first. Victor experienced a few fights at the start of the school year. He came home with a black eye one day and his mother asked, "What happened?"

"Oh, he called me a dirty Mexican," replied Victor.

"Well, what did you say to him?" Manuela asked.

"I didn't say anything."

"Well," she said, "you just continue to mind your own business and do what's right and you will win that person into being your friend."

It is little wonder that Victor still regards Lucille Lindberg and his mother as two of his truly outstanding teachers.

The Mark of Rodriguez

Victor's mother was a most amazing and exceptional individual. Everyone in Edna knew her as Manuela but many of her Mexican-American friends affectionately referred to her as "Meme." She was a small woman physically, only five feet plus two inches, but in many other ways she was a giant. Her light brown skin was accented by her black hair which now had several gray streaks running through it. Her dark brown eyes always reflected a gaiety and friendliness, and they were complemented by her soft, calm voice. The softness of her voice and her carefully chosen words were usually full of praise for anyone listening to her. Many Mexican-Americans, especially teenage girls, would come to her with their problems, knowing that their confidence would never be betrayed. Older women came too, for they respected her ability to direct and support her own family. Once in a while even men would stop by to ask Manuela for advice on how to avert a divorce. No matter how small or how serious the problem, Manuela had a gift for making people feel better about their world. The least anyone would receive in Manuela's home was an understanding ear and a cup of hot coffee. There was always a cup of coffee offered as a token of friendship as well as a traditional Mexican-American courtesy. Manuela was a gracious hostess and impressed people with her sense of good judgment and self-acquired wisdom.

She had no formal schooling, not even first grade, yet she was blessed with a kind of patience, tolerance, and wisdom which endeared her to all who came to know her. She had a spirit of enthusiasm and stamina matched only by her personal pride and character.

Manuela was a tremendously positive thinker and earned great respect and admiration in the Edna community. Everyone knew Manuela. She was very active in the PTA, and if you asked her something, she couldn't say, "I don't know," she would say, "Me don't know." But most importantly, she could communicate. She possessed the daring and audacity of a finished politician and had the patience of Job.

Manuela had been married twice. Her first marriage, in the early 1920s, was to a man named Feliciano Gaona. Everyone called him by his nickname, "Chano." Chano was a farmer in the rural community of McFadden, Texas. He was a short, somewhat stocky fellow who loved drinking and *ranchera* (Mexican country) music. He could play the guitar and often invited a couple of his friends who were also musicians to come visit on Saturday night or Sunday afternoon. Together they would form a *conjunto* which usually consisted of a guitarist, an accordion player, and a violinist. They would play and sing *corridos* and *rancheras* while their wives and children watched or danced.

Manuela and Chano were married for several years and they had four children, two boys and two girls. The boys were named Vicente and Esiquiel, and the girls were Rafaela and Theresa. Life on the farm during those days preceding the Depression consisted of a long workday from before sunup to well

(from left) Vicente Gaona, Manuela, Chico Gaona

after sunset. The music of the conjunto was truly a godsend. There was music, dancing, and laughter to lighten the spirit. It also provided the neighbors with an opportunity for conversation, exchanging news and good old *chismes* or gossip.

One Saturday evening Chano invited a friend named Augustine Rodriguez to come play with the conjunto. Augustine worked on a nearby farm on the outskirts of a one-store country town called Inez. He was a plowman and he enjoyed a reputation for being able to make the straightest furrow with a plow drawn by a team of two mules. He was also an excellent accordion player. His playing with the conjunto was an instant improvement and he soon became one of the star attractions. Augustine Rodriguez was divorced. He and his wife had four children, three sons and one daughter. The boys were Julian, Juan, and Desidoro. Maria, his daughter, had gone with her mother when Augustine and his wife divorced. The three boys remained on the farm with their father.

As the years went by, Chano began to go into town on Saturday nights. McFadden, which was just one country store, was only a few miles away. He began to drink more and more heavily. Augustine would drop by the farm on Saturdays and they would play and sing their corridos and rancheras. As Chano continued drinking, his relationship with Manuela became more and more distant and finally they were divorced.

No one is certain what happened next. What is known is that Manuela took Rafaela and Theresa with her and left the two boys with Chano. Soon after the divorce, she went to live with her relatives near Inez, and there in Inez Augustine began his courtship of Manuela. A year later they were married. Soon Manuela gave birth to a girl they named Adela. In 1932 they had a second child — a boy. They named him Victoriano but called him by the shorter name of Victor. A year and a half later, Manuela give birth to another girl, Frances. And so it was that Victor became a member of the Rodriguez family which consisted of his father, Augustine, Manuela, his mother, two older half-sisters, Rafaela and Theresa, and his own sisters Adela and Frances. In addition, he inherited a half-sister (Maria) and three half-brothers (Julian, Juan, and Desidoro) from Augustine's previous marriage.

Augustine continued to farm near Inez until he moved the entire family to a larger farm near Lolita where he died in 1936, when Victor was only four. This was the year that Manuela decided to move her family to Edna.

When they first arrived in Edna, Manuela found it difficult to find a job. The Depression still lingered in South Texas and jobs were scarce. One day she left her four daughters at home and took little Victor with her, and they walked into the well-to-do Anglo community and began going door-to-door asking about any kind of possible employment. Manuela was primarily interested in finding a job as a cook and house-keeper. The first day left them both tired, disappointed, and frustrated. They had spent the entire day knocking on doors and had not had anything to eat, though neither one of them would admit to being hungry. Time and again Manuela was told that no help was needed. The next day, they started out again. They made inquiries at two houses and met with the same results, but the third house they visited proved to be their lucky number. Manuela went to the door of the big two-story house and knocked. This was the house of Dr. R.W. Wells, a prominent physician. Mrs. Wells greeted them and Victor was impressed with her friendliness and ladylike manner. He had heard stories about how some of the Anglo-Americans treated their hired help and he said a silent prayer that this woman would hire his mother. Mrs. Wells talked to Manuela for nearly an hour and although Victor didn't understand what was said, he could tell by his mother's face that she had finally found a job. In the years to follow, Dr. Wells, his wife, and his family were to have a strong influence on Manuela in raising her family.

Victor's mother was a good teacher and she spoke to him often about responsibility, pride, and honor. "Many people take their names for granted," she would say in her soft, quiet voice. "The name of an individual is the most important title a person can have. One should always try to improve oneself so that it will reflect favorably on one's name. You can add other titles before your name such as Captain, Doctor, Reverend, or even Mister, but your own name will command the real respect that people have for you. Let people know that your word means something," she would continue. "If you tell someone that you will report to work at 7 o'clock in the morning, be there at 6:45 instead and people will soon come to respect your sense of responsibility by your personal behavior."

She could neither read nor write and her personal signature consisted of an X that required a witness and a counter signature. Victor remembered vividly an occasion when she affixed her X to an insurance policy. The young Anglo-American salesman had come to the house to sell Manuela some life insurance. He was a good-looking fellow, neatly dressed, and very impressed with himself and his extensive English vocabulary. Although he took a great deal of time explaining the terms of the policy, it was obvious that he was bored. He even yawned once or twice and made no effort to apologize. Manuela, as was her usual custom, served him a cup of coffee, but he pretended not to notice it and it remained untouched.

Victor was always amazed at how his mother, who could speak only a few words of English, managed to communicate with the Anglo-Americans. In important situations such as this one, she would ask one of her friends who could speak both English and Spanish to translate for her. The salesman made it a point to assure Manuela that her X was a perfectly legal and binding signature. He went on to remind her that the insurance company would expect her to honor her X as a commitment in every respect. The young man's behavior seemed to annoy Manuela, but she listened patiently and courteously to his every word, thus giving him the impression that she understood him fully. He asked her again if she understood the significance of her X as a binding signature. Manuela spoke to her witness and translator in slow but deliberate Spanish and asked that the following message be translated to the salesman: "There is nothing more sacred than one's personal signature. Some people can spell their name fully and are blessed with the grace to write it beautifully, yet they do not honor it. I can only make an X and though it may be lacking in grace and beauty, it represents dignity, pride, and honor. May it always be respected as the mark of Rodriguez."

First Christmas in Edna

While Victor was not certain about his mother's philosophy, he had a great deal of confidence and faith in what she did and said. In 1936 the Rodriguez family, like many others, still felt the stress brought on by the Depression. Manuela rented a small wood frame house in the heart of the Black community across the street from the First Baptist Church. This was the family's first exposure to Black people, and their ignorance provided them with a certain amount of suspicion and apprehension about "colored people." While the family managed to survive on Manuela's limited income, they approached the Christmas season with good health, but few, if any, prospects for Christmas gifts.

On Christmas Eve, the temperature plummeted to below freezing. All of the neighbors were burning wood in their iron kitchen stoves trying to keep their small homes warm. The night was clear with a full moon shining brightly on the roofs of the wooden houses. It had rained the previous day and the muddy streets were hardened by the freezing temperatures. The small drainage ditches on both sides of the street, which contained the run-off water, were also frozen solid. The little houses which lined the street did not have indoor plumbing. The only source of water was a faucet which stuck out of the ground about two feet high, each faucet serving four adjacent families. In anticipation of the hard freeze, everyone brought buckets and other containers and filled them with water before nightfall. They also availed themselves of a visit to the outdoor privies which were located in the backyards.

The Rodriguez family huddled around the wood-burning stove that Christmas Eve. As they sat chattering and laughing, they could hear the howling north wind and they felt it penetrating their small house through the cracks in the walls. They were about to go to bed when suddenly they heard footsteps on the front porch. It sounded like several people. There was a moment of silence, then a loud knock on the door, and many footsteps scurrying away into the darkness. Manuela and her family sat there silently for a while until they were certain that the people whom they believed to be pranksters or vandals had gone. Finally Manuela raised her finger to her lips and motioned to everyone to stay silent, and she tiptoed across the room and peeked through a crack in the door. With the kerosene lamp in one hand, she opened the door slowly, and as she did, the light from the lamp fell upon a bushel basket full of big red apples. Someone had left the basketful of apples on their front porch! A single red ribbon was tied around the yellow basket.

Manuela stayed up that night baking apple pies and making preserves. (Victor was left with a special fondness for red apples, especially during the Christmas season.) The children learned a great many important things that night. They learned not to judge people by the color of their skin. They learned to appreciate people for their actions and the sincere thoughts and kindness which stem from the heart. More importantly, though, they learned the lesson that Manuela had taught them about the basic goodness of people.

The next morning, Christmas Day, it seemed as if the entire neighborhood rose earlier than usual. As the sun came up the wind was still and although the temperature was slightly below freezing, it was a beautiful, clear day with not a cloud in the sky. The neighbors were busy sweeping their front porches and greeting each other with a wave and "Merry Christmas." Next door to the Rodriguez family lived the Pattersons, a Black family consisting of the parents, three boys and a girl. Mrs. Patterson came over and gave Manuela some peach preserves and Manuela gave Mrs. Patterson one of her apple pies. The Black minister of the Baptist church across the street came over and wished Mrs.

Patterson and Manuela a Merry Christmas. He handed each lady a shoe box which contained a dozen eggs and a small slab of home-smoked bacon. Mrs. Patterson gave him some peach preserves and Manuela gave him an apple pie.

Although there were no gifts exchanged among the Rodriguez family members that Christmas, they enjoyed a hearty breakfast to start off the day. Manuela made a stack of flour tortillas which she converted into tacos stuffed with scrambled eggs and bacon. Victor and his sisters had often eaten Manuela's tacos of potato and egg or bean and egg, but on this particular day, the bacon and egg tacos were an extra treat and it made the beginning of Christmas Day seem even more special.

After breakfast, Manuela warmed some water in a metal pot on the wood-burning stove in the kitchen. She went outside and brought in a round, tin, size-ten tub. She poured several buckets of cold water into the tub and mixed in some of the water she had heated on the stove. Two-year-old Frances got the first bath, then Victor, who was four. Next she told the three older girls to bathe themselves. After each child was bathed, the tub was carried outside and emptied. Even half full it took two people to carry it for it was three feet in diameter and two feet tall, with hinged metal handles. One person on each side would grab a handle, lift the tub, haul it outside, and empty it off the edge of the front porch. The last tubful of water was often used to wash clothes or scrub the floor.

On this beautiful Christmas day back in 1936, after they had bathed and dressed, Manuela, Victor, and the girls walked across the street to attend Christmas Day services in the Black Baptist church. They had not yet become acquainted with the Catholic Church. Besides, Manuela felt that by attending services in the Baptist church they could get to know their neighbors better. The Black minister greeted them at the entrance and escorted the Rodriguez family to the very front pew. He asked them to sit down — while the rest of the congregation stared curiously. As Victor looked around, he couldn't help noticing that he and his mother and sisters were the only non-Black people in the entire church. He didn't know whether to feel out of place or special.

The minister came to the front of the church and mounted to his pulpit. As he raised his hands, the congregation stood and began singing. This was Victor's first introduction to the Christmas carol "Oh Little Town of Bethlehem." After the singing of that first song, the minister said, "We have some very special guests with us this morning," and he introduced Manuela, and Victor, and his four sisters. Everyone in the audience applauded, and Manuela and her children beamed with pleasure. When the church services were ended, they walked outside into a sun-filled churchyard. All the neighbors shook hands with Manuela and she in turn said *"Gracias"* to each of them.

When they finally left the churchyard, Victor felt very good although he could not explain to himself exactly how he felt or why he felt this way. He also could tell, though his mother and sisters didn't say so, that they shared the same feelings. Was it the singing? Was it the friendliness of the people? Was it God trying to tell them something? Whatever it was, it certainly was a good feeling. They went home and spent a quiet day talking and sharing their first visit to a church in Edna. They ate their supper that evening and chatted around the stove until a little past eight o'clock. Then everyone got into their sleeping places — Manuela and Frances in one bed, Rafaela, Theresa, and Adela in the other. Victor slept on some doubled-up blankets on the floor next to the wood-burning stove.

When everyone was tucked in, Manuela, in her quiet voice, said, *"Gracias a Dios por este dia,"* and then, as she had done so often before, she added, *"Hasta mañana — con el favor de Dios,"* and she blew out the kerosene lamp.

Robert Barnes

World War II was little more than a year old when ten-year-old Victor made the transition from the Mexican-American school to the Anglo-American school. He was a little nervous about the change although Rafaela, Theresa, and Adela had already preceded him there. Rafaela was now a tenth grader, Theresa an eighth grader, and Adela was in the sixth grade. The girls had all made a generally smooth transition and had been well received in the Anglo school except for a few curious stares cast their way. They had been well prepared by Manuela who told them to be polite and to smile at everyone.

The fact that Victor had to repeat the fourth grade was of little concern to his mother. She felt that the most important thing was that he be allowed to continue his education. And besides, she reasoned, her girls had repeated the fourth grade and they were all doing fine in school. Manuela had a *dicho*, or saying, which helped her overcome all adverse or difficult situations. "*No hay ningun mal que por bien no venga*," she would say — "There is nothing so bad that something good can't come from it." Victor, like his sisters, felt that if it was all right with Manuela, then it had to be all right.

Victor's first teacher in the fourth grade at the Anglo school was Miss Whitely. During the first week she discovered that he was a very fast learner and she was impressed with the fact that he was well disciplined. He was polite and had a sincere curiosity toward learning, and he paid careful attention to everything the teacher said. She rewarded his efforts by providing positive reinforcement for his learning, and his spirits were raised considerably by her praise. When she discovered that he had some artistic talent, she would exhibit his drawings on the bulletin board. The other students accepted Victor as a regular member of the class and many were to become his lifelong friends.

While Victor gained the acceptance of the members of his fourth-grade class, other students were slower to make him welcome. They directly or indirectly reminded him that he was different and often poked fun at him. They would direct comments at him like, "Hey, *amigo*, are you lost?" or "Where is your burro?"

At lunchtime Victor took his brown paper lunch bag from under his desk, and he was conscious of the looks cast his way. Many of the students lived in the neighborhood and went home for lunch. Others brought a lunch box or bag with a sandwich of ham, bologna, or cheese. Victor would go outside and sit under a tree to eat one or two of Manuela's tacos. These were usually flour tortillas stuffed with refried beans and bits of salt pork bacon, or they might be filled with potatoes and eggs. While many of the students were curious about what Victor was eating, they limited their curiosity to directing a few stares his way. When he glanced up and caught them staring he would just smile at them, giving the impression that he was enjoying a terrific lunch. Little did they know how much he craved the luxury of a ham and cheese sandwich.

While Victor was not entirely comfortable in his new environment in the Anglo school, he was becoming more self-confident about it. He remembered some of the things Manuela had said about people in general. "People are basically good," she would say. "Just give them a chance and you will find that most people are good people." So far, everything was going just fine and Victor was convinced that his mother was right. And then one morning, after he had rung the church bell, he arrived at school early as usual, and was about to sit down on the steps at the entrance to the building when he noticed another boy walking onto the school yard. Victor had seen this boy before and as he came closer recognized him as Robert Barnes.

Robert was one of the students who seemed to always outdo the others in recess activities. He could run, jump, and throw as good or better than most, and he was a tough kid that even the school bullies left alone. Robert was mischievous and protected his own interests and opinions with a reputation of being able to handle himself in a wrestling match or even a fistfight. While he hadn't been branded as a troublemaker, Robert had had his share of referrals to the principal's office as a suspect in several fights. He knew that he was walking on thin ice and that another referral could result in a school suspension, or — even worse — a conference between the principal and his parents.

As Robert walked up the steps, he tripped on a step near Victor's left foot. He got up and accused Victor of tripping him. Victor called Robert a liar and stood up to face him. Robert didn't like being called a liar, and the boys grappled with each other and went tumbling down the steps to the ground. Robert quickly rose to one knee. He swung with his right fist and caught Victor under the left eye. At the same time, Victor, swung with his left fist and drew blood from Robert's upper lip. They were both shocked and hurt by the sudden pain and backed off to assess the damage.

Robert touched his upper lip, felt the wetness of blood, and saw it on his hand, and he shouted angrily, "You dumb Meskin, look what you did!"

To which Victor replied, "You dumb gringo, you started it!" He could feel his left eye beginning to swell.

Just as they were about to approach each other again, a car drove up and parked in the street about twenty feet away. Miss Whitely emerged from her car and approached them. She could tell that her unexpected arrival made the boys a bit nervous.

Noticing Victor's swollen eye and Robert's bloody lip, she asked, "Robert, what happened to your lip?"

Receiving no reply, she turned to Victor and asked, "Victor, what happened to your eye?"

Taking the cue from Robert, Victor did not reply.

"Were you boys fighting?" she asked as she handed Robert a handkerchief.

Robert and Victor glanced at each other and Robert quickly said, "We were just playing."

Miss Whitely was not ready to accept this explanation and she turned to Victor and asked, "What really happened here?"

"It's like he said, we were just playing," replied Victor.

"Well, go into the boys' restroom and wash your faces," ordered Miss Whitely, not sure they had told her the truth. As they were about to walk away, she issued a friendly warning, "You two stay out of trouble."

The boys went to the restroom and without speaking went about the business of washing and cleaning up. Before they had completely finished drying themselves with paper towels, a janitor walked in carrying a bucket and a mop, and then the bell rang and the boys went to their classrooms. They didn't see each other during the day except for a brief glimpse at recess. Although some of their classmates were curious about Robert's lip and Victor's swollen eye, none of them asked questions.

That afternoon when school was dismissed, Victor and Robert happened at the same time to walk out the door where their brief encounter had taken place that morning. They stopped at the top of the steps and looked at each other for a moment. Then, without saying a word, they walked down the stairs and went in separate directions as they headed home.

The next morning, Victor woke to the sound of the locomotive train engine as it passed near his house on its daily morning route at 4:15. He quickly got out of bed, dressed, and washed his face in the metal pan that Manuela had left near a bucket full of water on a small bench on the front porch. He ran the two miles to ring the church bell, and after serving as an altar boy for the five o'clock mass, he walked to school, going slowly since it was still early. His eye was a little swollen, but it didn't hurt as much as it had the day before and he had no mirror at hand to check it. He was unaware that the area surrounding his eye had turned a dark blue. He reasoned that since he could see okay and it was less painful it must be all right.

When he got to school, he sat on the steps near the entrance as usual. Although he didn't take any books home with him, he always conducted a mental review of everything he had learned the day before. Getting there early, he found these steps a good place for his review. When it was necessary for him to take books home to study, one of his sisters would bring them to school for him the next morning so he wouldn't have to carry them when he ran to ring the church bell.

He had finished his mental reviewing and was about to get up from the steps when he saw Robert walking toward the playground. He was carrying something under his right arm and as he came closer he stopped and kicked it high in the air toward the steps where Victor sat. The object rolled forward and came to a stop about ten feet from the bottom step.

Victor had never seen a real football and he sat there staring curiously at it. Robert stopped and waited a moment and when he saw Victor just sitting there staring, he yelled out, "Well, don't just sit there, kick it back!"

Surprised by Robert's invitation, Victor got up from the steps and picked up the football. He had never touched one before and he wasn't certain that he could actually kick it even if he wanted to, but he had seen Robert kick it and he thought it was worth a try. He took three steps forward and with a good running start he kicked the ball as hard as he could, sure that the ball would sail well over Robert's head. But he had underestimated Robert who back-pedaled while keeping his head and eyes on the ball above. The ball landed in Robert's arms and he kicked it back well over Victor's head.

Victor retrieved the ball and was about to make his second attempt, but before he could kick, Robert ran up to him and said, "Let me show you how it's done." He showed him how to hold the football with the laces turned up and how to drop it. Then as his foot came up to meet the ball, he whipped his leg up from a bent position into a straight, upward pendulum motion.

This was the start of a new routine, and Victor developed into a fair punter as he and Robert spent many mornings kicking the football back and forth. As time went by, they always tried to be on the same team during recess. They made it a habit to arrive at school early every day and they would pretend to be high school players on the football team.

Both boys came to school barefooted like many of the other boys in those days. There was a war going on and leather goods, including shoes, were rationed. Besides needing the money, you also had to produce ration stamps to buy a pair of shoes. No one could know for certain whether a person could not afford a pair of shoes or if they were extremely patriotic to the war cause. Anyway, Victor felt more comfortable going barefoot as did many of his classmates.

As Robert and Victor became better acquainted, they spent more and more time together. During the lunch hour, Robert would trade one of his ham sandwiches for one of Victor's refried bean and bacon tacos. It was through Robert's friendship that Victor developed a strong interest in football. Then some time in the middle of Victor's first year in the Anglo school, Robert Barnes began to be absent. Victor would get to school early each morning hoping that Robert would be there but a whole week went by and Robert didn't show up. Victor missed his friend and though he played with the other boys during recess, he missed the early morning fun with Robert. He was shocked to learn one morning that Robert would not be returning to school. Miss Whitely announced to the class that Robert had contracted a very serious case of pneumonia and had passed away the night before.

The next morning Victor arrived at school early and as was his habit, he sat on the steps at the entrance to the school. As he sat there, he remembered his confrontation with Robert. They could have become serious enemies, but instead they had become fast friends. It had all begun when Robert Barnes shouted out to Victor, "Don't just sit there, kick it back!" Victor remembered Robert's response to Miss Whitely's inquiry about his bloody lip and Victor's swollen eye. "We were just playing," Robert had said.

As Victor sat on the steps picturing again their first encounter and their ensuing friendship, he recalled his own response to Miss Whitely's inquiry, and he softly repeated out loud, "It's like he said, we were just playing."

The Saturday Night Dance

In 1944, Victor was promoted to the fifth grade in the Anglo school. While he had made many friends there, he still missed those from the Mexican-American school. Jesus Gonzales was his best friend and he had dropped out of school after the fourth grade. So had Jacinto Benavides, Mauricio Nava, Alberto Farias, Eduardo Nava, Julio Garza, and scores of other young Mexican-Americans who opted to work instead of continuing their education. A few of them became migrant workers following the cotton-picking season from Edna to West Texas. Others did the best they could at farm labor, chopping or hoeing weeds in the cotton and corn fields in the vicinity of Edna. Victor was caught in a quandary between his Mexican-American friends and his new-found Anglo-American friends.

After the war, the three sons of Dr. Wells — Frank, Sonny, and Pat — returned from their tours of duty in the armed forces and built a small cottage in their backyard for Manuela and her family. All of a sudden Manuela and her children found themselves living in the midst of the Anglo community. The small cottage was not the most spacious place the family had lived in, but it was new and it had a commode and a cold-water shower. The kitchen was small but it had an indoor water faucet. The configuration of the house was basically a rectangle. The bathroom and shower were on one end and the kitchen at the other. In between there was a small round table about five feet in diameter. Bunk beds were built on one side against the wall opposite the entrance. And for the first time, the family had the luxury of a home equipped with electricity!

While they enjoyed the small new home in the prestigious Anglo community, they were isolated from the barrio and their friends who lived in the Mexican and Black neighborhoods, but of course Edna was a small town and there was still ample opportunity to associate with friends and acquaintances. For instance, there was the dance held every Saturday night which all of the Mexican-Americans attended from eight in the evening until one o'clock Sunday morning. The dances were held on a covered platform about twenty feet by thirty feet, built about two feet off the ground. The platform had no walls, open on all four sides to maximize the cool summer breezes. The *musicos* or the musicians usually occupied the end farthest from the entrance of the *plataforma* or platform. Permanent benches were built inside the railing which consisted of one-by-four pieces of lumber nailed to the floor by four posts that supported the roof. Light bulbs hung from the crossbeams. The admission was usually one dollar for the male participants. Ladies were admitted free.

The females usually occupied the benches on the outer perimeter of the dance floor. The men stood outside on the ground until the music started. Then all the males would walk up the steps onto the raised dance floor and select a female to dance with. One of the "understood" traditions was that the females were to dance with all or any of the males requesting a dance. Except for extenuating circumstances, it was considered a deep insult to turn down a dance invitation. Even the married women honored a request for a dance from a male solicitor. Everyone knew which women were married and had jealous husbands. It was, by the same token, fairly well known to the women which husbands had jealous wives.

It was also well known that you should stay as far away as possible from anyone married to, or engaged to, or even acquainted with the Quijote brothers and the Panza brothers. These two families lived on farms and when they came into town on Saturday night they usually celebrated by drinking and dancing. They were also enemies dating back several generations. No one really knew when or why the feud had started, but one thing was certain — there was bad blood between the Quijotes and the Panzas. On more than one occasion, the rival brothers had taken turns inflicting stab wounds to each other in the middle of the dance floor. Needless to say, when the Quijotes and the Panzas appeared on the dance scene, a certain amount of tension filled the air.

Victor went to work at the A.A. Egg grocery store every Saturday at 7:00 a.m. He would begin by sweeping the inside of the store and then the outside of the entrance in front of the store. After that chore was done, he would put out all the fruit and vegetables and sprinkle water on them, which gave them a fresh appearance. About eight o'clock the customers would begin to arrive and Victor assisted the cashier by bagging and sacking groceries. About ten the farmers and ranchers began to arrive and business picked up; they bought food and provisions to last them for a whole week as most only came to town on Saturday. Victor was thirteen when he started working at the grocery store from seven in the morning to ten at night, and he earned four dollars a day. He was grateful that the owner of the store, Mr. Alfred A. Egg, had seen fit to give him the job. He was the first Mexican-American to work in a grocery store in Edna.

Somehow, slowly but surely, it seemed as if the Second World War had created a change in the way people felt and treated each other. The war had created jobs for women in nearby Victoria and Foster Air Force Base and at Aloe Field Air Force Base. Many of the young Mexican-Americans had joined up, and military service provided them an opportunity to travel to places they had only dreamed about. Victor's sisters also were able to find jobs at some of the clothing stores. Saturday was a very special day in the lives of the citizens of Edna. For those who lived and worked on farms it was their day to go to town. All of the businesses did well that day.

One Saturday before leaving for work, Victor heard his sisters discussing the dance that was to take place that night at the plataforma. They discussed who might be at the dance and they traded or agreed to lending or borrowing a skirt or a blouse. Sometimes wearing a borrowed garment would cost a sister the chore of washing dinner dishes for a whole week, but they always reached an agreement on borrowing or trading something suitable for the dance.

After listening to all the swapping, Victor ran to ring the church bell and serve as an altar boy for the early mass. Then he ran to the A.A. Egg grocery store and worked until 10:00 p.m. After putting in a fourteen-hour workday, he would go home and bathe. He usually arrived at the dance around 11:30.

It was his habit to lean up against an automobile as if he recognized the car as belonging to a friend, or he would sit in the car and watch the dancers enjoying themselves. Victor was popular with everyone but he didn't know how to dance. And after working at the store for fourteen hours he was too tired to even think of dancing. But it was his obligation as the only man in the family to go to the plataforma to escort his sisters and mother home after the dance.

On this particular Saturday night, Adolfo Hernandez had brought his car to the dance. Victor greeted Adolfo and received permission to sit in his car. During the course of the evening, the Quijote brothers drove up in their pickup and Juan Quijote, the youngest of the three, came over and began talking to Victor. He knew that Victor was still in school and he asked, "How are things going with the gringos?"

Victor answered that everything was fine, and Juan offered to buy him a drink. As the conversation continued, the Panza brothers drove up in their Model T Ford and parked on the other side of Adolfo's car. Richard Panza came over and said hello to Victor from the left side of the car where Victor was sitting, then added, "I'm glad to hear you're still in school. How do you like it?"

Victor said he liked going to school all right. Richard was one of the younger Panza brothers. Richard and Juan were nearly the same age, though Richard at fifteen was a year older.

Richard asked Victor if he could buy him a coke. Victor thought for a minute, feeling awkward because Juan had already offered to buy him a drink. He didn't want to offend either one of his friends. Besides, the older Panza brothers were still in their car just to his left and the Quijote brothers were parked on his right. He had heard of the knife fights between the two families, and he did not want to be caught in the middle of one.

Now the music became loud and some of the more intoxicated young men on the dance floor began yelling, "*Aye ha hay*" at the top of their lungs. The musicians were playing the corrido called "*El troquero*" which meant The Truck Driver. Both the Quijote and the Panza brothers got out of their cars and started in the direction of the platform.

As they walked away Victor stepped out of Adolfo's car and said to Richard and Juan, "Come on, I'll buy both of you cokes."

Richard and Juan were caught by surprise, and after hesitating a moment, they followed Victor into the *cantina* which was adjacent to the dance platform. Victor was relieved to have smoothed over the situation, but now another problem crossed his mind. Did he have enough money in his pocket to cover the cost of the drinks for the two boys? He put his hand in his pocket and began to feel the coins trying to judge the amount of money he had. When he was convinced there was enough, he pulled out his hand with the money and was relieved to see that he had a little over seventy cents worth of coins.

The waiter came over and asked, "What will it be?"

All three boys ordered cokes and when the waiter brought the drinks Victor was about to pay for them when Juan reminded him that it was he, Juan, who had invited Victor for a drink. To which Richard replied, "I invited him, too!" Thinking desperately for a way out, Victor suggested that since there were three of them they could flip a coin and the one with the odd face coin would buy the drinks. All three flipped their coins and covered them on the table with their right hand. Juan took his hand away and his coin showed tails. Victor removed his hand to reveal his coin with tails. Finally Richard moved his hand and his coin too showed tails.

The three boys laughed and Richard looked at Victor and asked, "Any more ideas, school boy?"

Juan suggested that since the first flip was a three-way tie they should flip again. Richard agreed and the three boys flipped their coins again and covered them with their right hands. In the meantime, the waiter came over and placed three bottles of coke on the table. Richard and Juan both removed their hands from their coins and both of the coins showed heads. Victor showed his coin and it too showed heads. By that time all three boys were laughing and everyone in the cantina was both surprised and interested in the flipping proceedings that were taking place—they were surprised because a Quijote and a Panza were sitting at the same table laughing instead of fighting, and they were interested because they did not know the name of the game the three boys were playing. A crowd gathered around the table and the boys became the center of attention. Both men and women began to place bets on which of the boys would flip the odd coin. The boys flipped once again and Victor's coin came up tails while both Richard's and Juan's coins showed heads.

Victor was about to pay for the drinks when Frank Herrera, who had placed a bet on Victor's coin said, "No, since your flipping the odd coin made me a winner, I will buy the drinks!"

"Now," continued Herrera, "let's bet again and see which boy flips the odd coin."

While all of the betting was going on, the musicians finished playing a corrido called "*Juan Charriasquiado*" and announced that they would be taking a fifteen-minute intermission. As the dancers were heading toward the cantina, their attention was drawn to a mob of people in the middle of the saloon.

"What's happening?" asked one of the spectators.

"It's the Panzas and the Quijotes . . ." was all that was heard as a partial reply to the question.

Hearing this, the three older Quijote brothers and the two older Panza brothers rushed into the cantina expecting to find their two younger brothers fighting. Amazed, they saw Richard Panza and Juan Quijote seated at a table drinking cokes and flipping coins. And to top it off, all three boys were laughing and it looked like they were having a good time. Carlos Panza was the first to break through the crowd surrounding the table where the three boys sat. Trine Quijote appeared on the opposite side of the table behind his brother Juan's chair.

"*Que pasa?*" asked Trine Quijote. Before Juan could answer, Trine noticed Richard Panza sitting across the table — but it was the same table where his younger brother sat! How could this be? Quijotes and Panzas do not share tables! Carlos Panza was as shocked to find his brother Richard sitting at the same table with a Quijote brother.

"*Que estas haciendo?*" Carlos asked Richard.

Richard looked at his older brother and said, "I'm just sitting here with my friend Victor."

"Me too," said Juan Quijote as if he could read his brother's mind. "I'm just sitting here talking with Victor."

Victor found himself surrounded by the Quijote and Panza brothers — an uneasy spot again.

"Who is that with your little brother?" a spectator asked Carlos.

"He is Manuela's boy," Carlos answered. "He's the one who rings the church bell every morning. He goes to school with the gringos. He's okay. Even the dogs like him."

Before the conversation could be carried any further, Sheriff Lewis Watson entered the saloon and worked his way through the crowd around the table. He looked at the Panza brothers and then at the Quijote boys.

"What's going on here?" asked the sheriff.

The Quijote and Panza brothers looked at each other and said nothing.

The waiter, a man of middle years, came over and said, "*Que tal,* Sheriff Watson?" When the sheriff once again asked what was going on, the waiter replied, "Victor was just teaching us how to play a new game he learned at the gringo school."

"Oh," said Sheriff Watson. "What do you call this game?"

"It's called *Cabezas o Colas,*" chimed in Trine Quijote, trying to sound intelligent.

"What does that mean?" asked the sheriff, casting a suspicious eye on Trine and looking at Carlos Panza from head to toe.

Carlos knew the sheriff was visually searching him and he slowly took his right hand out of his pocket where he had been fondling a switchblade knife. He put his hands on the shoulders of his little brother sitting in front of him. "*Cabezas o Colas,*" began Carlos, "means 'heads or tails'."

The waiter chimed in again and explained, "The real name of the game is Odds."

The sheriff was about to say something else when the musicians started playing a tune called, "*El Gavilan.*" It was a corrido and everyone welcomed a fast piece of dance music, especially after an intermission that had been extended by peoples' interest in the Odds game. As if they needed an excuse to put some distance between the Quijotes and the Panzas, the crowd rushed back to the plataforma and began dancing.

The Panzas and the Quijotes were the only ones remaining around the table where Victor and the younger brothers sat. The sheriff asked Victor if it was true that these boys were friends of his.

Victor said, "Sure, Sheriff, I've known them ever since we were in first grade. I also know your son Lewis. He is in my fifth-grade class."

"Yes," said the sheriff, "I've heard of you. My son says that you're a pretty smart young man. I have also heard of Manuela, your mother, and she is a fine woman." Then he asked Victor if his mother and sisters were here at the dance and Victor said they were and added that he had come to escort them home after the dance.

The sheriff looked at the Quijote and Panza brothers, turned to Victor, and said, "I'm glad you're taking care of your mother and sisters." To the Quijotes and the Panzas he added, "If your younger brothers are friends of Victor, they must be okay. You older boys behave yourselves. I wouldn't want any harm coming to anybody at the dance." He turned, walked out the door, and waving at the people on the dance floor he got in his car and drove away.

As the music continued, Trine Quijote turned to his older brothers and said, "Come on, let's go show them how to dance." Then he turned to his young brother and asked, "How about you, *manito*? Are you coming?"

"No," Juan said. "I'm staying here with my friend Victor."

"Me too," said Richard Panza, "I'm staying here with Victor."

"*Entonces vamos a bailar*" (Then let's go dance), said Carlos Panza and then he added, looking towards Trine Quijote but speaking to his own brothers, "Let's stay out of trouble — at least for tonight. I wouldn't want any harm to come to anyone at the dance."

With that, both sets of brothers left the cantina and went to the plataforma. Victor, Richard Panza, and Juan Quijote stayed at the table drinking their cokes and watching the dance through the windows of the cantina.

At one o'clock the musicians played "*La despidida*" ("The song of departure," "the last dance" or "good bye"). At the end of the dance, the crowd applauded and said good night. As people began to leave, Victor, Richard, and Juan walked outside the cantina. Victor waited for his mother and sisters while Richard and Juan waited for their brothers.

Trine Quijote came over and shook Victor's hand and said, "I'm glad

my little brother has a good friend like you. I hope you do well in school."
With that the Quijote brothers got in their pickup and drove off.

Carlos Panza came over and shook hands with Victor too and said,
"Richard tells me you are very smart. I hope that someday you will graduate from high school." The Panzas got into their Model T Ford and
drove off.

Victor's mother, Manuela, and his four sisters, Rafaela, Theresa,
Adela, and Frances, came out and they all started walking home. It had
been a long day for Victor. He had gotten up at four-thirty that morning
and ran to ring the church bell, served as an altar boy for the early mass,
and worked at the grocery store from seven o'clock in the morning until
ten at night. Manuela put her hand on his shoulder and asked if he was
tired.

"No," replied Victor, pride building up inside him. He was, after all,
the only man in the family and he took great pride in escorting his
mother and sisters. He wouldn't want any harm to come to them on the
way home.

A Year of Transition

In the fall of 1947 Victor had many friends in the Anglo-American school. In early September he enrolled as an eighth-grade student in the junior high school. Victor couldn't understand why there was a policy against speaking Spanish in school — there was no one else there that he could speak to in Spanish, even if he wanted to. As the only Hispanic in the eighth grade, Victor had no choice but to speak English and he soon became proficient with it.

Without realizing it, though, he was gradually losing his fluency in Spanish. At home, his sisters spoke English to each other and to him. They lived in an Anglo community, they attended the Anglo schools, and they worked in stores owned by Anglo-Americans. The only time they spoke Spanish at home was when Manuela was present, but even Manuela would insert a word or two in English during the family conversation. More and more, as time went by, the Rodriguez family was assimilating to the ways of the Anglo-Americans.

After the first week of school, the junior high coach, Aubrey Stallings, announced the start of football practice. The notice posted on the bulletin board stated: "All 8th graders interested in playing football report to the gymnasium after school next Monday." Victor's spirits soared! Ever since Robert Barnes had introduced him to football in fifth grade, he had had a deep interest in the sport.

During the 1944 season, Edna High School had fielded a fine team and won the regional championship in the Class A Division. Victor attended all the home games with his older sisters, and he learned the names of every one of the players on the Cowboy team. There were three sets of brothers — Tommy and Lynn Dunham, Bruce and Bobby Strane, and Gene and Stuffy Greene. Dave Curlee was the quarterback and Albert Thurmond one of the guards. There were two Hispanics on the team who had transferred into the Edna school system from elsewhere — Narciso Lopez played tackle and Robert Molina was an end. Winning the regional championship elevated the entire team to hero status in Edna. They had achieved the ultimate goal possible in their sport.

Victor and all of the eighth graders saw themselves as successors to the "Team of 1944" as they were affectionately referred to in Edna. The youngsters didn't realize how extremely difficult it would be for another team to accomplish the same goal. Most of them had only played touch football during recess in elementary school, or flag football during physical education classes in junior high, but they all dreamed of one day playing "real" football and wearing all of the equipment that football players wore.

Monday was a very long day for the boys in the eighth grade, waiting for classes to end, but finally they gathered in the gym where Coach Stallings greeted them and gave instructions on how to put on their football equipment. Many of them had difficulty walking around in their football shoes which had cleats on the bottom, but they had all seen the high school boys perform and they pretended they were perfectly comfortable wearing them.

Next, Coach Stallings took them out to one of the practice fields. He talked to them about working hard and always putting forth their best effort. He spoke about playing fair and about always exhibiting good sportsmanship. Then he put them through a series of exercises and running wind sprints, which would be the pattern day after day in preparation for the beginning of the season. These eighth graders had played touch football and attended the high school games; they had cheered for their heroes and dreamed of someday becoming heroes themselves, but this kind of physical practice was something that none of them had experienced. There were times when they questioned whether they would survive the agony, although the doubts were not spoken aloud. Outwardly, they were the picture of self-confidence, poise, courage, and strength. When they went home in the evening, they were physically worn out and had only enough strength to eat supper and go to bed. In the meantime, they still had to attend classes and perform tasks at home.

By the end of the first week of practice, each eighth grader was placed in one of the eleven offensive positions of the football team. Victor was put at center and it was his responsibility to snap or center the ball backward to the quarterback at the start of each play. Although this was not the position that he had wanted to play, Coach Stallings convinced him that it was a very responsible spot because every play was started by his snapping the ball on the prescribed count or signal. Victor had always pictured himself as the player who ran a hundred yards with the winning touchdown with the final seconds ticking off the clock, but Coach Stallings insisted he was the best man for the center position, so Victor decided that he would perform to the very best of his ability as the center.

In the meantime, Victor still had his "individual civic responsibility" to perform each morning as the church bell ringer. Despite the fact that he was sore and every muscle in his body ached, he still woke up at the sound of the train each morning at four fifteen and as he ran to ring the church bell, he would pretend that the barking dogs were football opponents and he would sidestep them as if he were a broken-field runner weaving his way toward a touchdown. He was full of hope and sometimes his imagination and his dreams of being a hero almost seemed real. And although his dreams were shattered when they suffered a dismal defeat of 36 to 0 by the Yoakum Bulldogs, Stallings somehow managed to rebuild their confidence prior to every game. The junior high team played five games that fall and they lost every game by lopsided margins. They turned in their equipment at the end of the season, and although they were disappointed, they vowed that next year would be better.

By this time in the school year, some of Victor's Hispanic friends were returning to Edna from their cotton-picking excursions in West Texas or from the beet fields in Ohio. Some of them had managed to save a little money to see them through the spring of the following year when they would once again work in the cotton fields and cornfields chopping or hoeing weeds. A few managed to find work in service stations pumping gasoline and washing cars. Still others worked as dishwashers in the restaurants or did yard work or other odd jobs.

Victor managed to maintain his relationship with some of his Hispanic friends at the Saturday night dances or Sunday church services. Meantime, he continued to work in Mr. Egg's grocery store on Saturdays and on his ranch on Sundays. It was a large ranch and there were always plenty of fences to mend. Once Victor put in fifty-two new fence posts and Mr. Egg paid him ten cents per post. That was a hard day's work and it netted Victor $5.20 working from sunup to sunset. In addition to the money he earned, Victor acquired a reputation as a hard worker who always did a good job. Soon, other Anglos were trying to hire him to work for them, but Victor was a loyal employee and he always gave preference to Mr. Egg.

The spring semester went by fast and Victor decided to try his hand at picking cotton during the summer. Farmers were offering four dollars per hundred pounds of cotton and he was sure that if he really committed himself to the task he could out-pick just about anyone, and he proved it the first week. But at the beginning of the second week, a truckload of Mexicans from below the border arrived and they could outdo everybody. Victor had been picking between two and three hundred pounds of cotton per day. He did his absolute best to pick more, but he just couldn't top three hundred pounds a day. But then Victor had not yet met Don Pedro, an elderly cottonpicker from Chihuahua.

Don Pedro could pick cotton faster than anyone Victor had ever known. He was about five feet eight inches tall, and lean almost to the point of being skinny. He began to notice Victor in the cotton fields and to take an interest in him. They briefly exchanged greetings while weighing their cotton at the trailer which carried the scales. Victor decided to position himself as close to Don Pedro as possible in order to learn some of his trade secrets. The first thing he noticed was that Don Pedro used two sacks. He dragged one behind him and when it was half full he would leave it lying in the furrow. Then he used his second sack, which had been rolled up and strapped to his back, as he continued to pick in the same direction he had started. He completed the row and turned back, picking till he reached the spot where he had left his first sack only half full. He emptied the contents of his spare sack into the original one, and in this way he didn't have to drag a heavy load behind him and he could move forward much faster. Besides, as he later explained to Victor, "It's less tiring on your legs."

Victor also noticed that the old man had a small bell which was attached with a four-inch shoe lace to his belt. As Don Pedro moved forward, the bell made a continuous ringing sound, keeping cadence with his steps. Victor asked why he carried the bell tied to his belt, and Don Pedro explained that the bell made just enough noise to warn the snakes that he was coming. "If you have to worry about the snakes, you cannot concentrate on picking cotton," he explained. "Most snakes will get out of your way if they know you are coming."

Victor was impressed by the wisdom of this old man who could pick more cotton than anyone else in a single day. No one knew for certain how old he was, for not even Don Pedro knew his real age and he could only speculate that he was around seventy. He had determined his age based on some historical recollections that people had associated with his birth date, give or take three or four years.

The wise old man taught Victor that if you really want to succeed at anything then you have to be committed and focused. He pointed to some young Mexicans who had come up from Mexico and said, "You see those *muchachos* over there. They are talking to each other constantly instead of picking cotton. The others are singing together and they are more interested in their singing than picking cotton. They are not committed to their job. If you want to pick cotton fast, pretend that every boll of cotton is a coin, like a nickel or a quarter, and that you would like to pick as many of the coins as you can. Do not think or daydream about anything else because that will destroy your concentration."

Victor took Don Pedro's advice seriously and the next day showed up at the cotton field ready and eager to pick cotton. He had managed to find a small bell stored in one of the cabinets of the Catholic Church where he rang the big bell every morning. He reasoned that since the little one was dusty it had been on that shelf for a long time, so he decided to borrow it and return it after the cotton-picking season was over. He also had a spare sack which he strapped to his back in the same fashion as Don Pedro.

That morning Don Pedro asked Victor to pick cotton in the row next to him. The old man had brought two sticks about three feet long. Each stick had a hook made of heavy wire attached through a hole drilled at one end. The stick could be attached to a person's belt by the heavy wire hook. Victor was curious about why the stick was necessary, but before he could question Don Pedro the old man saw the questioning look on his face and explained, "Some snakes are not as easily frightened as others. If you should run into a stubborn snake, use your stick. Besides," he went on as he handed one of the sticks to Victor, "it's always a good idea to be prepared."

"Now," said Don Pedro, "let's go pick cotton."

Victor started picking in the row next to Don Pedro and for a while he was able to keep pace with the old man, but after some two hundred yards, Don Pedro was thirty feet ahead of him. Noticing his absence, Don Pedro turned and called back, "Remember to stay focused and to concentrate." When they were about halfway down the row of cotton, they stopped to leave their half-filled sacks and began filling their spare sacks. By the time they were at the end of the row and ready to turn and pick in the opposite direction Victor was within ten feet of Don Pedro.

"You're doing fine," said Don Pedro.

They reached the spot where they had left their first sacks and emptied the contents of the spares into them. When they continued picking, Victor was amazed at how light his empty sack was, strapped over his left shoulder and dragging behind him. By this time, it was almost mid-morning and the sun was getting very hot. Don Pedro and Victor were sweating profusely and some of the white poisonous insecticide which had been sprayed on the green cotton plants had rubbed off on their hands and clothing. The sweat from their bodies and the insecticide produced a strong odor under the blazing heat of the day.

By the time they reached the end of the row, the trailer with the weighing scale had arrived. Don Pedro turned to Victor and said, "Leave your spare sack of cotton here so they can weigh it, and while they are weighing and emptying our sacks we will go and bring the others." They tied the open end of the cotton sacks, flung them over their shoulders, and hurried to the trailer to weigh in. Don Pedro's cotton weighed 206 pounds, and Victor's weighed in at 201.

By this time it was almost noon and most of the cottonpickers were taking a lunch break. Don Pedro turned and said to Victor, "If you want to stay here and eat, go on and stay. I am going to continue until I have picked over 400 pounds. Besides, you cannot pick much cotton with a full stomach." Victor decided to copy Don Pedro and they followed the same procedure in the afternoon that they had practiced that morning. By the end of the day, Don Pedro had picked a total of 425 pounds while Victor had picked 413 pounds. No one else in that cotton field had picked over 350 pounds.

When the cotton-picking season was over in late August, most of the pickers from Mexico returned home. A few of them, including Don

Pedro, were headed out to West Texas to continue picking cotton. The day before the Mexicans left for West Texas, Don Pedro and Victor sat down at the end of the day to eat their long-overdue lunch. They were both tired and they smelled of sweat and insecticide. Don Pedro complimented Victor for his commitment in becoming a good cottonpicker. "You will always succeed if you continue to have the same commitment that you have shown while picking cotton." He took off his small bell and handed it to Victor. "Take this bell and keep it as a reminder of a friend who once picked cotton with you. May it also serve to protect you from the snakes in the world."

Victor took off the bell which he had borrowed from the church and gave it to Don Pedro. "This bell is from my church and it has been blessed," Victor said as he shook hands with Don Pedro. "I will take your bell and place it in the church as a reminder to say a prayer for you."

The next morning Victor arrived at the church early to ring the bell. Afterwards he went to the storage cabinet and placed the small bell on the shelf. For many years to come, Victor would rise early each morning to ring the church bell, and once in a while he would go to the shelf where he had put the small bell with the leather strap, and he would dust it off. The little bell made a clear, distinct sound when he rang it, different from the sound of other bells. As he stood there in the bell tower of the church he would remember Don Pedro encouraging him to stay in school. As he put the little bell back on the shelf he recalled his old friend saying, "You will always succeed if you continue to have the same commitment that you have shown while learning to pick cotton."

Victor never saw or heard from Don Pedro again, but once in a while when cottonpickers from Mexico came through Edna during the summer, they would speak about a strange old man who could out-pick them all. Their reason for considering him strange was because he was a loner who seldom spoke to anyone. And they were especially mystified by the constant sound of a little bell which he always wore on a little leather strap tied to his belt.

Making the First Team

After spending a long hot summer in the cotton fields, Victor was ready and eager to return to school. He gave his mother some of his earnings and bought shoes and clothing for himself. It had been a profitable season and it felt good to have some money in his pocket. But although he was pleased with his success as a cottonpicker, he was relieved when the cotton crops had been exhausted in the vicinity of Edna. He was certain that there had to be a better way of earning a living than picking cotton. Besides, he reasoned, his teachers and everyone else he knew were encouraging him to stay in school.

His teachers had all emphasized the importance of a good education. His mother had insisted that he and his sisters continue their schooling. His best friend, Jesus Gonzales, who was leaving to follow the cotton picking season into West Texas, had advised him to stay in Edna and continue his schooling. And, of course, there were the boys who had played football with him in the eighth grade who were encouraging him to return to school and try out for the varsity. So Victor decided that his best choice was to return to school. Besides, the thought of playing football still appealed to him a great deal. He was anxious to try out for the squad. As a freshman, he knew that it would be difficult to make the varsity but he was determined to give it his best effort.

In mid-August of 1948, twenty-eight boys reported for football workouts. There was only one boy on the team who had played with the famous Cowboy team that won the regional championship in 1944. He was Tomeleigh Dunham, the quarterback of the current team. He had been the center on the team of 1944 when he was a freshman. This bit of information was very encouraging to Victor and he reasoned that if Tomeleigh could make the varsity squad as a freshman then so could he.

Tomeleigh was a senior now, along with Charlie McDowell, who was an outstanding runner as a halfback. Charlie's younger brother, "Babe", was a sophomore who was already showing promise as a passer and runner. Other outstanding performers were Fred Psencik who played guard and William Putnam, a running back. Bob Stovall was a sophomore who played end and was becoming a great receiver. The team worked very hard during the two-a-day practices and there were times when Victor wondered whether playing football was really as much fun as everyone had claimed. But then again, anything was more fun than picking cotton. Besides, the veteran lettermen on the team exhibited so much manliness and mental toughness that Victor didn't dare show any sign of weakness for fear he might not make the varsity squad — or even worse, he might be cut from the team.

The very thought of not being on the team made him more determined than ever, and he did everything he could to attract the attention of Coach Zimmerman. When the team was told to run four laps around the track, Victor was the first to finish — way ahead of the pack. His daily routine of rising early and running two miles to ring the church bell had benefited him beyond his own imagining. When the rest of the players finished running their four laps they found Victor standing there waiting without even breathing hard. Many of the boys were gasping for air while others were bent over or on their knees. They were amazed at how Victor could stand there unfazed and calm. But then they did not know about his early morning two-mile jaunt with all of the dogs barking at him en route to ringing the church bell.

Coach Zimmerman took notice of Victor's physical condition and assigned him to lead the team around the field, running warm-up laps before practice every day. Victor didn't want to be accused of showing off so he slowed his pace to lead the team around the field instead of running off and leaving them behind. The members of the team knew this and they voiced their appreciation to him for not making them look bad in front of the coach. Their behavior was a little confusing to Victor. He appreciated the fact that he could clearly excel in running laps so that Coach Zimmerman had appointed him to lead the team around the football field. And he appreciated the fact that the entire football squad was indebted to him for slowing the pace so as not to make them look bad. But on the other hand, the coach was always urging him to do his very best. Even while picking cotton, Don Pedo had, in his own way, urged Victor to be committed to the task at hand and to always do his best. Trying to balance the problem, he decided that for the time being he would be satisfied with the fact that he was in front of the squad and that both the coach and the team considered him a leader. Besides, he had the satisfaction of knowing that he could still do much better.

The football season of 1948 began with a non-district game against Rosenberg which was played on Friday night in Rosenberg. The day before the game, Coach Zimmerman announced the starting lineup. Tomeleigh Dunham was the quarterback. The running backs were Charlie McDowell, Robert Nairen, and William Putnam. The linemen were Weldon Bonnot at center, Fred Psencik and Perry Campbell, guards, Bob Stovall and Bill Miller, ends, and Cecil Reynolds and Victor Rodriguez, tackles. Victor was thrilled to make the starting lineup and he was excited about the game to be played the next day.

He had difficulty falling asleep that night, and when he finally dozed off, it seemed as if it was only a few minutes before he was awakened by the whistle from the train. He rose quickly, washed his face, dressed, and started running to ring the church bell. There was dew on the grass and the sandy loam street was damp. The wind was still, but there was a coolness in the air that made him feel good as he jogged the two miles to the church. It seemed to him that even the dogs were more active as they ran out to the middle of the street to greet him as he made his way down the dark street. Although they barked at him, he knew that the dogs knew him and that they were anxious to be acknowledged by the first human being they saw that early each day. As the dogs ran out they would bark and run along with him for a few yards. Some were friskier than others and they would jump up and touch Victor with their front paws. He greeted them by name and gave them friendly pats on the head. The dogs would retreat to their houses and Victor would continue down the street greeting and patting other dogs.

After ringing the bell and serving as an altar boy for the early morning mass, Victor jogged to school and arrived early as usual. He sat on the steps at the main entrance to the high school waiting for other students and teachers to arrive. As he sat there thinking about that night's football game, he recalled his friend Robert Barnes and the dreams they had shared about playing football in high school. He vowed to himself that he would play extra hard that night in memory of his friend who would not be there.

The other students began to arrive. Some came walking from their nearby homes, others arrived by bus from the surrounding farms and ranches. A few were driven by their parents in their post-war automobiles. As they arrived, they all greeted Victor as he sat on the steps at the entrance to the school. They congratulated him on having made the starting lineup. Others wished him good luck for the game that night. It seemed to Victor that although he had made a great many friends among his classmates, many of them he had never met were extremely outgoing and friendly towards him. All of this, it seemed to him, had happened overnight. It was as if they were saying to him, "You're a part of our football team, therefore you're a part of us."

Then to top it off, there was a huge pep rally with the entire high school student body present in the gymnasium. The pep rally took place right after the bell rang which usually meant that everyone should report to their first-period class, but today all of the students were going toward the high school gym.

Bob Stovall, an end on the football team, came up and greeted Victor and said, "Come on, Vic, let's go to the pep rally."

When they entered the gym all the members of the football team were directed to seats in the three rows of folding chairs set up in the front. The gymnasium served as a basketball court as well as an auditorium. In the back there was a stage which faced the front entrance. The band and the cheerleaders were already on stage. The student body stood in back of the three rows of chairs where the football team sat.

As the students came in, the band was playing the school fight song. It was the same as Notre Dame's fight song. The football players had goose bumps all over them. When the fight song ended, F. D. Ray, the high school principal, came to the microphone and asked everyone to stand for the playing of the national anthem. They remained standing and recited the pledge to the flag. Mr. Ray then introduced Bascom B. Hayes, the school superintendent. Mr. Hayes was always very neatly dressed in a suit and tie and he was a very articulate speaker. He spoke to the student body about the trip to Rosenberg that evening. He made a special appeal to everyone to practice good citizenship and good sportsmanship, and reminded them that they were the visiting guests and that anything short of good behavior would not be tolerated. He spoke to the football team about the tradition of the Edna High School Cowboy football team and their reputation for being tough, clean athletes who always exhibited good sportsmanship and great character. He closed his remarks by saying he felt certain that if everyone gave their best effort the score would take care of itself. The crowd cheered and applauded as Mr. Hayes walked off the stage holding up two fingers in the V-for-victory sign.

When Mr. Ray introduced Coach Zimmerman, the entire student body erupted into a loud roar. It was obvious that the coach commanded a great deal of respect and admiration from everyone there. He was one of Edna's most popular citizens.

Coach Zimmerman urged the student body to attend the game in Rosenberg. "We need all the support we can get," he said. Then he introduced the members of the team, beginning with Charlie McDowell and Tomeleigh Dunham who were the team captains. As he introduced the other members of the starting lineup, he would mention each player's name, their grade, and the position they played. The students applauded after each player was introduced. When Victor was introduced, Coach Zimmerman mentioned that he was the only freshman to earn a place on the starting lineup. Standing there with the student body cheering loudly, Victor experienced his first sense of what it was like to receive public recognition. Even his own teammates stood and applauded him with the rest of the student body. He stood up for a moment, his pleasure mixed with some embarrassment at all of the attention.

After the assembly was over, everyone went back to their classes, but for Victor the normal routine of returning to class was never again the same. Every student he met seemed extra friendly now, as if they were seeing him in a new light. They would make it a point to congratulate him and wish him well in the game that night. He was embarrassed by the attention, but at the same time both proud and happy. In all of his classes that day both students and teachers seemed to pay more attention to him than they had in the past. They all expressed their pride in him for having made the starting lineup and assured him they were going to Rosenberg that night to see the game.

It was difficult for Victor to concentrate in class and he wished the day would pass quickly. His mind wandered as he kept thinking about the game. If they ran a play in his direction, would he be able to tackle the ball carrier when he was playing defense? And when his team had the ball on offense, would he be able to carry out his blocking assignment? Would he perform as well in an actual game as he had in practice? His nervousness grew and he could hardly wait for the day to be over and the game to start.

After classes were dismissed, he went home. The coach had told them to eat a light meal before the game so he ate a bowl of soup Manuela had left for him. He was not very hungry due to his nervousness and anxiety about the game, but he knew he had to eat in order to have enough energy to play that night. After he finished the soup he started back to school.

Rosenberg was about a two-and-a-half hour drive from Edna and the coach had told them to be at the gym by four o'clock. They were traveling to Rosenberg by cars owned by some of the residents of Edna. The band traveled in the yellow school bus, and the football equipment was being transported in a pickup volunteered by another Edna citizen.

The cars carrying the football team and the bus carrying the band formed a caravan heading out on Highway 59. As they drove through town, all the stores were closed and many of Edna's citizens joined the caravan. Friday night's football game was the center of attention and the biggest event of the week. Victor rode in a car which belonged to Weldon Bonnot's dad. Weldon was a second-string center on the team. He was also a freshman and a classmate of Victor's. The other three occupants in the car were Babe McDowell, William "Putter" Putnam, and L. J. Korenek. They were all sophomores. Mr. Bonnot drove a 1948 Oldsmobile, a four-door sedan which featured a Dynaflow automatic transmission. It was the most luxurious car Victor had ever seen, much less ridden in. This also was the first time Victor had been this far away from Edna. He had previously been to Victoria, twenty-five miles west on Highway 59; the trip to Rosenberg was in the opposite direction, east on Highway 59 and 78 miles from Edna. This was the most excitement Victor had ever experienced in one day. And the football game was yet to come!

When the caravan arrived in Rosenberg, the band and some of the fans in their private cars stopped in town for refreshments while the football team went on to the stadium. The game was scheduled for eight o'clock and it was already 6:45. Coach Zimmerman instructed the team to go into the dressing room under the stadium, suit up, and be ready to go by 7:15 p.m. Then he had them sit in a circle on the floor of the dressing room. He stood in the middle and once again read off the names of the players on the starting lineup from his clipboard.

"This is the first game of the season for us," he began, then looked directly at Victor as he added, "For some of you, it's the first game you have ever played as a member of our varsity. If you go out there and play hard, play fair, and do your best we will win this game!"

Victor could feel a cold chill running through his body and he wished that they could run out on the field and play the game right now! The coach called on Charlie McDowell and Tomeleigh Dunham, the captains, to lead the team out of the dressing room and onto the football field for warm-up drills.

As the team walked out of the dressing room you could hear the clattering of the cleats of the football shoes as they shuffled their feet on the concrete floor, and they could hear the bands playing and the crowd cheering. The two captains led the team onto the field and the Edna fans erupted in a loud chant. "Cowboys! Cowboys! Cowboys!" they yelled. There were twenty-eight players on the team and as they ran out on the field, they formed a circle to do calisthenics. The two captains stood in the center of the circle and led them through their routine exercises, chanting in unison, "One, two, three, four." After they finished their calisthenics, they formed two lines on the left and right sides of the team captains who began to throw them short passes as each line released a player down the field.

While they were executing this drill, the game officials came over and introduced themselves to Coach Zimmerman. They asked to have the team captains from Edna meet at the middle of the football field with the captains from Rosenberg for the flip of the coin. Coach Zimmerman told the rest of the team to go wait on the sideline where they all knelt on one knee. They watched the captains and the officials flipping the coin to see which team would kick-off and which would receive. Rosenberg won the toss and decided to receive. The captains trotted over to the sidelines and joined the rest of their teams. The officials blew the whistle to signal both teams to line up for the start of the game.

Tomeleigh kicked off the ball to the opposing team. Victor and the rest of the Cowboys ran downfield in pursuit of the receiver who was attempting to dodge and weave his way upfield. Fred Psencik was the first tackler to hit the runner from Rosenberg. Fred hit him with his right shoulder and knocked him off balance. Before he could regain his balance, Cecil Reynolds hit him squarely from the left side, and both the runner and tackler went sprawling on the ground. On the next play, Victor tackled the quarterback for a five-yard loss behind the line of scrimmage and all of his teammates came up and slapped him on the back. As Victor waited for the opposing team to break from the huddle, he couldn't help noticing that he was the only Hispanic on that entire field. Rosenberg's team was composed solely of Anglo players and he was the only Hispanic on the Edna first team.

The game itself was a very hard-fought battle. Rosenberg led at half-time by six to zero, but Edna came back and tied the game in the second half, and the final score was a 6-6 tie.

After the game, the team caravan stopped at a restaurant to have their customary after-game meal. One by one the cars carrying the members of the team arrived and parked on the main street of Rosenberg. All of the players and the people who drove the cars went into the restaurant. They were all seated, five individuals to a table, when a man wearing a coat and tie came over and spoke with Coach Zimmerman. The coach called the two team captains over and spoke with them. Charlie McDowell and Tomeleigh Dunham then went around the room and gathered all of the juniors and seniors into an empty space in the farthest corner of the room. Then, one by one, the junior and seniors with the rest of the team in tow left the restaurant and returned to their cars. The juniors and seniors seemed to know what was happening, but the freshmen and sophomores were mystified.

The caravan of cars drove on until they reached El Campo, a small town about halfway between Rosenberg and Edna. They stopped at a restaurant, and while Coach Zimmerman and the two team captains went inside the rest of the team waited outside. After a while, Charlie McDowell and Tomeleigh Dunham came outside and Charlie said, "It's okay, we can eat here. It's going to take a little while for them to set up tables for us. They were about to close but they'll take care of us."

It was almost midnight and most of the players were starving, but the meal they were served was well worth the wait. Seated five to a table, each player received a plate with a huge chicken fried steak plus mashed potatoes, gravy, green beans, and hot rolls. They also had iced tea and a large slice of apple pie topped with ice cream.

During the rest of the trip back home the caravan of cars drove slowly through the early morning fog toward Edna. Most of the boys fell asleep with the consolation of knowing that although they had not won, they had not lost. Victor, the freshman, had not run the football back a hundred yards for the winning touchdown with time running out as he had imagined while dodging the dogs each morning, but he was proud of the fact that they had played a good game. After all, Victor reasoned, it was only the first game of the season with eight more still to play. Besides, he had achieved one of his personal goals — earning a starting berth on the first team.

Although Victor didn't realize it at the time, he had earned a great deal more. The reason the team had not eaten in the restaurant in Rosenberg was because the owner had a practice of not serving Mexicans in his restaurant. The juniors and seniors on the team had voted unanimously that if the entire team could not eat there then none of them would eat there. And Victor was now a member of the team.

Beeville Track Meet

In the spring of 1949, during his freshman year in high school and after the football season was over, Victor got to know Luther Zimmerman on a personal basis, and the coach would share his leftover newspapers with the youngster.

One day Victor was reading his newspaper and noticed a picture of a runner. He asked, "Coach, what's this picture all about?"

"Well, this young man is the defending champion from Karnes City, Texas."

Victor read the story of the young fellow who ran two miles every day, to and from home, and that he was preparing to compete in the district meet the following Saturday, which was three days away. And then Victor remembered what Lucille Lindberg had said when he was in that Mexican-American school — how she would always start the day by saying, "This is America, and if you prepare yourself and if you are willing to compete, you can be anything that you want to be." And Victor thought to himself, *If he prepares himself by running four miles a day, and I run six miles every day, I think that I am prepared to compete against him.*

So the next day Victor said, "Coach, I can tell just by looking at this picture that I can beat him." Victor was just an ignorant kid — didn't have the good sense to get butterflies.

The coach answered, "Well, I'm taking some typing students and some slide rule students to the UIL meet in Beeville this Saturday, and if you care to go, you're certainly welcome to join us." This was the University Interscholastic League which sponsored statewide competition in all areas of education.

Victor figured maybe the coach thought he was joking. That Saturday morning he ran two miles to the church and rang the bell. Then he ran a mile to the high school to catch the bus for Beeville — and all this on the same day as the track meet.

They arrived at the meet in Beeville and the coach, who also taught business courses, said, "I have to go register the slide rule contestants and the typing students.""You go lie down under that huisache tree and I'll come get you when it's time."

So Victor did just that. Eleven-thirty rolled around and he was getting hungry. The coach had left him with a quarter and said, "There's a restaurant up the street. If you get hungry, go get something to eat." So he did and he paid nine cents for a hamburger with all the trimmings. He had a Big Red and a piece of lemon pie. He didn't know anything about diet or nutrition; all he knew was that he was hungry.

When Zimmerman returned, he said, "They're announcing the second call for the mile run. Are you warm?"

And since it was 95 degrees, Victor said, "Yes."

"Well, you've got to report to the starting line." So Victor did.

The contestant from Karnes City was there with a flashy black and orange uniform. His bright hair had earned him the nickname of "Red."

Victor reported to the starting line, and the coach asked, "Did you bring your shorts?"

Victor answered, "No, sir."

"Well, roll up your blue jeans." So Victor rolled his jeans up as high as they would go.

The coach asked, "Do you have a T-shirt?"

"No, sir."

The official said, "Well, if you don't have a T-shirt, you can't run because you've got to have a number pinned on that shirt."

Coach Zimmerman had been a football player at Baylor University. He was six feet tall and weighed over 200 pounds. Victor was six feet tall and weighed 155 pounds. The coach took off his T-shirt and handed it to Victor, and it draped down over his shoulders like a nightgown.

"Tuck it inside your blue jeans," he was told, and he did but it still looked awkward.

The official pinned a number on Victor and said, "They're gonna give you three commands: on your mark, get set, and then the gun."

That was an unusual track in Beeville. It went immediately in front of the stands, and then instead of circling around in front of the other stands it went behind the stadium, so if the audience wanted to see the entire race, they would run to the top of the stadium and look down behind it. Many of them were not that interested; they knew that Red, defending champion, was there. He had run the mile in 4:58 when he set the record the year before so he was bound to win again.

When the gun was fired, they all started running. Although Victor knew nothing about racing, he noticed something interesting. He was used to running in the middle of the street in Edna when the dogs were chasing him, so he got into the middle of the pack and was leading going into the backstretch. But on every curve, Red was catching up to him because he was running in the inside lane like you do if you know what you are doing. But he was a good sport, and he exercised sportsmanship when he yelled to Victor, "Run in the inside lane, it's a shorter distance."

Now while Victor had been waiting under that huisache tree for the race to start, the coach had told him that if anybody talked to him, be nice to them.

Victor asked, "Well, what will I say to them?"

The coach said, "Well, ask them where they're from."

So Victor ran up beside Red and asked, "Where you from?"

As he was puffing, Red replied, "Karnes City."

They continued to run around that awkward track with the fans cheering for Red and laughing at the barefoot boy in blue jeans running beside him.

As they entered the final lap, Red and Victor broke away from the rest

65

of the pack and on the final turn they sprinted the last 100 yards to the finish line. Red broke his old record by a full two seconds and finished with a time of 4:56, but this time he finished second. Victor ran the first competitive mile of his racing career in 4:52 and established a new district record, to the astonishment of all the spectators and a very surprised Coach Zimmerman.

Victor winning the mile at the Beeville Texas District Meet, 1949

All kinds of stories began to spread about that race in Beeville, Texas. One of the most widespread tales was the story about how Ol' Red had been defeated by a young Mexican-American who had come out of the stands, rolled up his jeans, and — standing barefoot — had challenged and beaten him. They didn't know about all of the preparation Victor had as a church bell ringer with all those dogs chasing him every morning.

The next week, the *Edna Weekly Herald* sent to all of the business establishments three-by-five-inch cards with four words:

MANUELA'S BOY BREAKS RECORD

Though these small cards were also used for local death notices, Victor couldn't have cared less! This notice marked one of the proudest moments of his life!

*   *   *

During his junior year in high school Victor was named to the all-district football team as a tackle on offense and defense. After football season, he read some stories and books about the great Jim Thorpe and the famous miler named Glen Cunningham. Coach Zimmerman had assigned the track coaching duties to a new man, Albert Thurmond, who had been a star football player on the 1944 regional championship team. Coach Thurmond mistakenly entered Victor in the half mile instead of the mile at the state track meet, and in 1950 he finished second at the state meet behind the record-breaking effort of Paul Sentif from Brenham.

Manuela had a saying for when things were not going right: *"No hay ningun mal que por bien no venga."* "There is nothing so bad that something good can't come from it." And at the end of each day, no matter whether it had been a day filled with a lot of good events or many negative ones, she always expressed her hope for a better day when she blew out the kerosene lamp and said, *"Hasta mañana – con el favor de Dios."*

Two Sides of the Coin

During the summer of 1950, Victor was still working in Mr. Egg's grocery store and on his ranch when business was slow in town. He looked forward with great anticipation to his senior year in high school. After his personal accomplishments in football and track in his junior year, he was one of the most popular young men in Edna. Everybody in town now knew him by his own name, although a few of the older folks still referred to him as "Manuela's boy."

Talk among his classmates centered around their plans after graduation. Most of them expected to get a job and then get married. A few talked about going to college. Victor's main objective was just to graduate from high school, go to work, and support his mother. He had never in his wildest imagination thought about going to college, but some of his friends kept suggesting that his athletic ability could earn him a scholarship, especially if he improved his performances during his senior year. It was something to think about. He began to dream of an outstanding year as an athlete during this next year. While deep inside he had no real intentions of going to college, he let himself become involved in talk with some of his friends who were going. He kept telling himself that, after all, it was only a topic of conversation, and anyway it was nice to share in the talk.

One day, before the fall semester began, Coach Zimmerman drove up in front of Victor's house with some shocking information. He told Victor that he would not be eligible to participate in athletics during his senior year. Because he had transferred from the Mexican-American school after his fourth-grade year and they had made him repeat the fourth grade in the Anglo school, he was a year too old to take part in athletics in his senior year!

Victor was devastated by this news. He couldn't imagine not being allowed to participate in football and track during his last year in school. "If it's any consolation to you," Coach Zimmerman continued, "Perry Campbell and Franklin Marek are also ineligible to participate. I'm sorry to bring you such news. I've enjoyed working with you, and you have been a real asset to our team. I'll miss you a lot, but I hope you'll come back and finish your final year of school anyway."

The coach left and Victor stood there in a state of total disbelief and confusion. How could he just go to classes with no sports? It was his interest in football which caused him to go to high school in the first place, and it was his success in track which had kept him interested in school during the spring. He was so disappointed that at that particular moment he thought about dropping out of school entirely. Beside, he reasoned, it would be kind of nice to go to work full-time and earn some money.

As August approached, some of his friends became aware of Victor's ineligibility for football. His old friend Jesus Gonzales came by the house one Sunday on his bicycle and invited Victor to go swimming in the Navidad River on the outskirts of Edna. Victor hopped on the handlebars of Jesus' bicycle and they went down a back road to the river. Jesus parked his bicycle under an old oak tree which served as a landmark for them whenever they went swimming in this old river. They went upstream along the riverbank until they came to a bend where a five-foot cliff overlooked a pool about ten feet deep. They took off their clothes and Jesus jumped from the small cliff into the river feet first and landed right in the center of the deepest part. He went under water and made certain there was no danger of logs lodged below the surface. Then he yelled to Victor, "Come on in. The water's great." Victor took a running start and jumped in feet first.

In contrast to Victor's poor ability in the water, Jesus was an excellent swimmer. He took to it like a fish and he could swim faster than anyone Victor had ever seen. The only human Victor had ever seen swimming faster than Jesus was Tarzan. But then he suspected in the movies Tarzan was aided by the speeding up of the cameras. There was no doubt in his mind that Jesus was a faster swimmer than Tarzan. It saddened him that Jesus had not gone beyond the fourth grade. Jesus could have been a great athlete if he had stayed in school.

After they were tired swimming, the boys lay on the sandy surface below the five-foot cliff. Jesus had some news for his friend. "I'm going to join the Army and see other parts of the world, Vic. I don't want to go on picking cotton for the rest of my life."

"When are you leaving?"

"Next month, just as soon as the cotton picking season is over."

"Maybe I'll go with you"

"No," said Jesus, "you need to stay here and graduate next year."

"But they won't let me play football anymore, and I can't run track either. It isn't any fun just going to school if I can't play football and run track."

Jesus was quiet for a while and then he said, "You need to go back to school. There have been many times when I wished I'd stayed in school instead of working all the time. You have done a lot for us by staying in school and playing football and running track. Everybody knows you. And what will people think if you quit now? They'll think you weren't smart enough to finish high school! Besides, you can always join the Army after you graduate."

Victor didn't know what to say so he just lay there thinking about their friendship through the years. Jesus had always rejected Victor's encouragement to stay in school himself, and now here he was discouraging Victor from joining the Army and encouraging him to stay in school!

After a while, the boys got up and walked to where they had left Jesus' bicycle. When they reached the road Jesus asked Victor if he wanted to ride on the handlebars.

"No," said Victor, "I think I'll just walk or run for a while." He walked along the old dirt road while Jesus pedaled his bicycle slowly beside him. Neither boy said a word. Then suddenly Victor started to run. Jesus, pedaling his bicycle faster, pulled up beside him and they went side by side for a half mile. The faster Victor ran, the faster Jesus pedaled until Victor became totally exhausted.

When they finally stopped to rest, Jesus was the first to speak. "You know what," he began, "you're even faster than I thought you were. It's too bad you can't run in high school but it's not the end of the world. Go back and finish school. You're not a quitter. Besides," he added, "when you finish high school you can get a better job."

Victor was tired and confused, but deep inside he knew that Jesus was right. He knew that Jesus was truly his best friend and that he would always tell him the truth — even when he didn't want to hear it. Without answering, Victor hopped up on the handlebars and they went up the dirt road that led back to town. At Victor's house he jumped off the bicycle before it stopped and Jesus kept riding, but he yelled back, "Stay in school!"

Victor stood there watching his friend disappear around the corner. Jesus had gotten in the last word. And although Victor was disappointed that he and Jesus would not be joining the Army together, he knew that the advice was right. After all, he was his best friend.

Coach Eddie Shinn

When he walked in the house, Manuela told him that a man from Victoria had been there asking about him.

"What man?" Victor asked. "I don't know anyone in Victoria."

"This man wants to speak to you and he will be back here at six o'clock to talk to you in person," said Manuela, her voice filled with excitement. She had prepared supper and she wanted Victor to eat before the man returned. "But first," said Manuela, "you must take a bath and change into some clean clothes."

"Who is this man?" Victor probed further. "And what does he want with me?"

"I could not understand everything he said," replied Manuela, "but he said something about a good opportunity for you. He said he would be back, so hurry and take a bath and eat before he returns. I could tell that he is a very nice person. He even asked if he could have one of my tortillas!" she added proudly. "And he said I make very good coffee!"

Full of curiosity, Victor hurriedly bathed and ate, then went outside and sat on the front porch to wait for the man who was looking for him. *Maybe he'll turn out to be an Army recruiter,* Victor thought to himself. Then he could join the Army and really surprise Jesus! He sat there for ten minutes, and just one minute before six a very shiny, new Ford sedan came up the street and parked in front of the house. A distinguished-looking gentleman emerged and walked up to the porch where Victor sat. He wore a gray suit with a white shirt and tie. His shoes were polished, and Victor was impressed with his prosperous appearance. He was about five feet eight inches tall, and while he was not thin, neither was he fat. He came forward and extended his hand toward Victor.

"My name is Eddie Shinn," he said, firmly grasping Victor's hand.

"I'm Victor Rodriguez," Victor replied, trying to sound just as impressive.

"Oh, I know who you are," said Shinn. "I've heard a great deal about you ever since you ran in that track meet in Beeville. And I watched you run in the state track meet in Austin this past spring. I'm here to invite you to run at Victoria Junior College. I'm the track coach and I'd like to have you on our track team."

Coach Eddie Shinn

Victor was astonished and explained to Shinn that he still had a full year to finish high school and that he was ineligible to compete in track during his senior year.

"Don't worry about that," Shinn said. "If you register for one course at Victoria Junior College, you can finish high school here in Edna and compete as a member of our team on weekends." Then he went on, "You are a fine athlete and it would be a shame for you not to take advantage of this opportunity."

Victor was floored! He had thought that his athletic days were over and now, out of the clear blue sky, an opportunity had been presented to him! He shook hands with Eddie Shinn and agreed to participate in track at Victoria Junior College while still a senior in Edna High School.

* * *

In the fall of 1950, Victor returned to Edna High School to complete his senior year. During the football season he and Perry Campbell were named football managers by Coach Zimmerman. In the meantime, Victor also registered for a class in physical education at Victoria Junior College in order to be eligible to participate on the track team. During the fall he would work out on his own, running three to five miles of cross-country. Of course, this was in addition to his daily routine of running to ring the church bell each morning. He still continued to work in Mr. Egg's grocery store on Saturdays and on his ranch on Sundays.

One Friday in October, Shinn invited Victor to the Victoria College campus to compete in a two-mile run against some of the other members of the cross-country team. Victor took the bus from Edna to Victoria, 25 miles west on Highway 59.

As the bus approached the outskirts of town, Victor saw a sign saying Victoria Junior College was one-fourth mile to the right. The bus driver stopped and let him off the bus, and he walked the quarter mile to the college campus and asked directions to the gym.

Coach Shinn was waiting for him and took him to the dressing room to introduce him to six other runners who were members of the cross-country team. The coach told them all to suit up and get ready to run. After changing clothes, Victor went outside and began to warm up by jogging a very slow half mile on the grassy course where the two-mile cross-country run was to take place. It was a flat grass course laid out in an oval.

As the time for the race grew near, Victor performed some stretching exercises as some of the other runners came over to join him. And now Victor experienced something he hadn't known before. He was a little nervous at first and then his stomach felt as if it were full of butterflies. He couldn't understand what was happening. Was he nervous because this was his first competition of the year? Was he nervous because this time it was at the junior college level? Was it because he didn't know the abilities of his competitors? Would they beat him and make him look bad in front of Eddie Shinn? What was their background? Were they former high school state champions?

He didn't know what to do about the apprehension he was feeling so he decided to take the initiative and do something. He walked over and began to mingle with three of the runners who were warming up near him. He knew nothing about them, but somehow he had sized them up as likely the top distance runners among the six that were to compete that afternoon. They were Billy Seiler, George DeVillanueve, and Jimmy Stewart. Remembering the old advice from Coach Zimmerman, Victor began the conversation by asking, "Where are you fellows from?"

"I'm from Karnes City," said Billy Seiler.

"Victoria," said George DeVillanueve.

"Fort Worth," said Jimmy Stewart.

"Glad to meet you," Victor said, trying not to show any of his nervousness. And then he added, "I'm from Edna."

"Have you been working out every day?" asked Billy.

"Yes," replied Victor.

"What kind of workouts have you been doing?" asked George.

"I run about three to five miles a day," said Victor. Jimmy kept silent and Victor felt that he was sizing him up. Suddenly it struck Victor that these three runners were just as apprehensive about him as he was about them! He began to feel less nervous now and his confidence in his own ability was restored to a great degree.

Coach Shinn blew his whistle. Victor and the other three joined the group, and Shinn explained to them, "It's one mile around the course so you'll have to go around twice. The course is marked with a white chalk line. Just stay to the right of the white chalk line. I will give you your times at the end of the first half-mile, at the mile mark, and at the mile and one-half mark. Our track manager will record each of your individual times at the end of the two-mile run. Any questions?"

The seven runners stood silent. Coach Shinn took out his starter's gun and told them to take their marks. When they were ready at the starting line, he fired his gun and they were off and running. Jimmy Stewart took the lead with a long, smooth even stride. He was followed by Billy Seiler and George DeVillanueve. All three were familiar with the course. Victor ran right behind George and he could hear the other three runners just behind him.

As they approached the middle of the first curve, about a quarter mile into the race, Victor again experienced a feeling totally foreign to him. His nervousness vanished and a new sensation took control of his entire mind, body, and soul. It was as if his mind was issuing a strong, silent message to every muscle and fiber in his body. "*Stay close!*" his mind said silently. "*Don't let them get away. What are you doing back here?*" He strode comfortably past George and pulled even with Billy who was running two strides behind Jimmy. "*That's better,*" his mind encouraged him. And "*Stay right there,*" as they approached the first half-mile.

Jimmy, Billy, and Victor went past the first half-mile on the backstretch of the oval. Coach Shinn called out the time as Jimmy Stewart passed him, followed closely by Billy Seiler and Victor. "Two minutes, fifteen seconds," shouted Coach Shinn. As the first three runners went past the half-mile mark, they could hear the coach calling out the time of the other runners behind them. "Two minutes, twenty seconds . . . two minutes twenty-five seconds," he shouted. As the last of the seven runners went past him, Coach Shinn began walking briskly across the open course to station himself at the mile mark. Victor's mind began talking to him again. "*Keep it up, you're doing just fine,*" his mind was saying.

As they rounded the second turn, and entered the straightaway in the direction of the mile mark, it seemed to Victor that the pace had slowed a little. Jimmy was still two strides ahead of Billy and Victor, who were running side by side. "*The pace is slowing up a little,*" his mind was saying to his body. "*Pull up alongside Jimmy and stay on his outside shoulder.*" As Victor moved up, Jimmy glanced slightly to his right to see which runner was coming up to join him in the lead, cutting his eyes to glimpse Victor without turning his head.

Jimmy Stewart was from Fort Worth. He had been an outstanding miler in high school and had been recruited by North Texas State. North Texas was a track power in the state and at the national level as well. Jimmy had enrolled at North Texas State as a freshman in the fall of 1950. He had competed well during the month of September as a member of the cross-country team, but because of an over-abundance of distance runners, North Texas opted to farm him out to Victoria College. Jimmy was a conscientious young man who had high aspirations to be a top distance runner. He had worked hard as a member of the Paschal High School track team and had earned a reputation in the Fort Worth area as one of the top milers in that part of the state. He had accepted Eddie Shinn's offer to come to Victoria Junior College because he felt he could be very competitive at this level. He planned to improve his performance, and thereby earn a return scholarship from North Texas.

After another quick glimpse at Victor, Jimmy stepped up his pace a little. The runners were now approaching the mile mark and they could hear Eddie Shinn calling out the time as each second ticked off on the watch he held in his hand. When they were ten yards away from the end of the first mile mark, Shinn called out a time of four minutes forty-four seconds, and as they ran past the first mile mark he called out four minutes forty-five seconds. Jimmy and Victor were now leading Billy Seiler and George DeVillanueve by a little more than twenty yards. The other two runners were some thirty yards back.

Victor's mind was seriously concentrating on the race. It kept telling his body that he was doing fine. *"Stay relaxed and keep up your rhythms between your arms and legs,"* said his mind. *"At the end of the first half mile your time was 2:15. At the end of the mile your time was 4:45, which means that your second half mile was 15 seconds slower than your first half mile."* Victor had trailed Jimmy, Billy, and George during the first half mile. Now he had pulled up even with Jimmy and his mind kept telling him that he was doing fine. He was breathing evenly and his legs felt a little heavier, but he was able to maintain a good, consistent, even stride.

His mind began to speak to his body once again. *"When you get to the middle of the next curve, pick up the pace a little."* Jimmy continued to run shoulder to shoulder at Victor's left side, right next to the white chalk line. As they approached the curve and began to turn to their left, Victor was on Jimmy's outside right shoulder. When they approached the middle of the curve Victor's mind said, *"Pick up the pace now!"* His body and legs responded instantly.

Jimmy was surprised by Victor's action, but he reacted by increasing his own pace quickly, thus keeping Victor running outside his shoulder while he maintained the position close to the chalk line. Victor's mind was trying to analyze what was happening and spoke to his body and legs once again. *"Don't let him keep you on his outside shoulder around the curve! He's forcing you to run farther by making you run a wider curve. He's testing you! Test him right back before you finish this curve or he'll beat you the next time on the final curve."*

Victor reacted to his mind's advice and accelerated to a faster pace. Now he was running faster, but he was still running smoothly and maintaining a good rhythm between the movement of his arms and knees. His acceleration took him past Jimmy and he was leading by a full two strides around the rest of the curve before entering the back stretch. Jimmy, realizing what was happening, tried to increase his own pace, and though he was able to do so, he had difficulty maintaining his rhythm between arms and legs. His arms were swinging across his chest instead of back and forth on either side of his body. He began a galloping effort and bobbled up and down instead of striding smoothly as he had done at the start. He was breathing more heavily, an indication that he was extending himself close to his maximum limits. Victor told himself that he needed to be patient. *"Don't panic!"* his mind told his body. *"You still have more than a half mile to go. Just stay as close as you can until you turn into the final straightaway.*"

The two front runners, Victor and Jimmy, had now widened the distance between themselves and the next two runners by more than fifty yards. They were in the backstretch approaching the one-and-a-half mile mark. As the runners came by, Coach Shinn called out their times.

"Seven minutes thirty seconds," Coach Shinn shouted as Victor and then Jimmy ran past him. The next time he called out was seven minutes and forty-five seconds, so Victor and Jimmy knew they had a fifteen-second lead on the nearest runner behind them. With a half mile to go, Victor once again experienced a new feeling. His legs were getting heavier and try as he might, he had a difficult time breathing evenly. His mind began to speak to his body again. *"You have less than a half mile to go. You're tired, but it will be over before you know it! Jimmy is going to try to beat you, but he looked tired when you passed him. Chances are he is more tired than you are."* As the runners came to the last curve, Victor found himself running closer to the white chalk line. *"Now is the time to really move out,"* his mind said. *"Don't wait until the home stretch — do it now!"*

Victor's entire body reacted instantly in response to his mind's command. He found himself able to accelerate even faster, and with the excitement of coming off the final curve into the home stretch his mind said, *"That's it — keep it up — you're in the lead and you can win the race!"* He could no longer hear Jimmy's footsteps behind him and he knew that he was totally in control of the race. He was now just 200 yards away from the finish line and he could see Coach Shinn checking the time on his stopwatch. His mind was now telling him to pick up the pace even more. *"Give it all you have."* His legs responded and he broke into a hard, all-out sprint. He crossed the finish line about one hundred yards ahead of Jimmy, the only runner close to him. The others finished a distant eighty to one hundred yards behind Jimmy. Victor was tired, but the victory seemed to rejuvenate his whole body.

Jimmy came over and congratulated him and said, "You sure looked good today." As he was shaking hands with Jimmy, the other runners came over and patted him on the back and congratulated him.

"Thanks," said Victor still breathing a little unevenly. Coach Shinn came over and all of the runners gathered around him. He announced that Victor's winning time was nine minutes and forty-five seconds. All of the runners applauded and Victor stood there basking in his new moment of glory.

"This is the first practice race of the year," Coach Shinn reminded them. "I'm proud of all of you and if we continue to work hard, we'll have a fine cross-country team."

After the team had showered they left to go to their dormitory. Jimmy Stewart was the only one to remain with Victor in the dressing room. He came over and sat next to Victor who was tying his shoes. Jimmy spoke in his quiet voice and said, "I hate to get beat by anyone, but if I had to lose to anyone, I'm glad it was you."

Victor didn't know what to say so he extended his hand and Jimmy grasped it firmly. Without another word, Jimmy turned and walked out of the dressing room leaving Victor all alone. As he sat there on the wooden bench by himself, Coach Shinn walked in.

"Good," he said, "I'm glad you're still here. Come on and I'll take you home."

"You don't have to do that," Victor replied. "I can catch the bus on Highway 59. I hate for you to have to drive that far just to take me home."

"Don't you worry about that," said Coach Shinn, "I have plenty of time. And besides, I want you to tell me all about your first race in that track meet in Beeville."

The First Visit to College

Since he was now a senior and many of his classmates were still encouraging him go to college, Victor decided to explore the possibility of continuing his education. His second-place finish at the state track meet had attracted the attention of several colleges and universities, and he received letters from many of the track coaches inviting him to come visit their campus. Eddie Shinn spoke to him often about the kind of future he could have when he completed his college education. "You're having a good cross-country season, Vic, and all of the hard work and training will really pay off for you when we enter the regular track season in the spring. And next year will be even better when you enroll here as a full-time student."

Victor liked Coach Shinn, an easy-going man who seemed to understand Victor's situation. He saw the dilemma in his struggle to decide whether to get a job after graduation or go to college. If Victor went to work he could substantially help his mother and the rest of his family, even with a limited income. If he decided on college, his mother would have to continue to work hard and make sacrifices to support herself and the family. And besides, there was no guarantee that Victor would succeed as a college student.

The only other Mexican-American from Edna who had gone to college was Abraham Trevino. Like Manuela, Mrs. Trevino had lost her husband when her son was young. Abraham had served in the Navy during World War II, and since his discharge Uncle Sam was paying his way through college with the G.I. Bill. When Victor first heard about Abraham's good fortune, he wished that he had an uncle who could provide him with money for college. He later learned that "Uncle Sam" meant the government of the United States and that the G.I. Bill was a program for veterans to go to college.

When Abraham was granted a furlough during his tour of duty in the Navy, he came home to see his mother, and also visited Victor's older sisters, Rafaela and Theresa. By the time of his release from the Navy he was a mature man in his mid-twenties, but the fact that Victor knew him personally was an encouraging factor which helped him deal with his personal dilemma. It was the kind of encouragement Victor needed to at least explore the possibility of college.

He discussed the situation with Coach Shinn who suggested that Victoria Junior College would give him several advantages, especially its closeness to Edna. "You would be near your home and you could visit your family on weekends. If you think this is where you want to go, I can make arrangements for you to visit one day next week. Do you know what field of study you want to enter?"

"What do you mean?" asked Victor, totally confused.

"You know," said Shinn, trying to give Victor credit for knowing something about which he obviously knew nothing, "a field of study is a specialized area of study that you would major in."

"Major in?"

"Yes. A major is the subject you would concentrate on such as engineering, agriculture, music, English, art, or speech," said Coach Shinn, trying hard not to confuse him any further.

"Art," replied Victor, with renewed interest. Miss Lindberg had taught him art in the Mexican-American school and he had kept up his interest and skill. This year, Miss Meadie Pumphrey, the high school yearbook sponsor, had named him editor and artist for the yearbook. "I want to study art," Victor told Coach Shinn.

"Good," said Coach Shinn, "but before you decide that you want to major in art, let me make arrangements for you to visit the head of the art department."

"The head?" asked Victor.

"Yes. That means the person in charge of the department. If you like, I can arrange for you to talk to Miss Ethel Thurmond, the art department head."

Victor agreed to return next week to meet Miss Thurmond.

The following week, the Victoria Junior College track team was competing in the Texas Relays Track Meet which was held annually in Austin. The meet was on Friday and Saturday, so Shinn told Victor to come to the campus on Thursday morning and he would have time to visit the art department before leaving for Austin.

Victor arrived on the Victoria College campus around 9:00 a.m., and the coach had made the arrangements for him to visit Miss Thurmond. He told Victor to go up to the second floor and handed him a piece of paper with Miss Thurmond's name and room number. Victor found the room and the door with a metal plate which read, "Art Department." He opened the door and entered a large classroom. This was the back of the room and the students were seated two to a table facing the front, but hearing the door open they all turned around and looked at him. Victor stood there in silence as his eyes searched vainly for a teacher.

Seeing the curiosity of the students, he said nervously, "I'm Victor Rodriguez and I'm looking for Miss Ethel Thurmond."

"She's in the storeroom baking some pottery in the kiln," one of the students said and added, "She should be back in about ten minutes."

With that, the students turned their attention back to their art tasks. That is, all except one — a tall slender girl with long brownish-black hair and fair skin. She remained facing him while half standing and half sitting on the stool beside her drawing desk. She smiled at him. There was a sparkle in her eyes, and the smile revealed beautiful pearly-white teeth. It was only when she spoke that Victor detected an accent which made him suspect she was not Anglo-American.

"Are you a new student?" she asked.

"No, I'm just visiting the art department today to explore my field of interest," replied Victor, using the same words spoken by Coach Shinn in an effort to sound intelligent. She left her drawing table to come over and introduce herself.

"I'm Florinda Reyes," she said. "I've seen your picture in the paper, but I've never seen you on campus."

"I'm still a senior in high school," Victor explained. "I want to attend college here after I graduate and Coach Shinn suggested that I visit the art department and speak with Miss Thurmond."

"She's very nice," Florinda said. "Where are you from?"

"I'm from Edna," replied Victor. He felt an immediate attraction to this tall, slender girl. who seemed to go out of her way to make him feel at ease. She was pretty, friendly, and uninhibited, and her natural beauty matched her glowing personality. She spoke with an accent which also enhanced her charm. He was grateful for her conversation as he had felt awkward standing there in silence.

A middle-aged woman came in and introduced herself. "I'm Ethel Thurmond and you must be the young man Mr. Shinn told me about," she said as she extended her hand to greet Victor.

"Yes, ma'am, I'm Victor Rodriguez," he answered as he watched Florinda return to her table.

"Let's go over to my desk and talk," said Miss Thurmond.

They walked to the front of the classroom and Miss Thurmond sat in her chair behind the desk, motioning for Victor to sit facing her. She told him about the art program and the course offerings. As they talked, the bell rang and the class gathered up their books and other belongings and left. Victor was listening to Miss Thurmond as she continued to talk, but he was feeling a strong urge to turn around and see if he could get another look at Florinda.

Finally the teacher asked Victor if he had any questions.

"No. I think I really would like to come here next year and be in your art program."

"I've heard some very nice things about you from Coach Shinn," said Miss Thurmond. "I would be happy to have you in my class."

"Thank you," said Victor, and he told her goodbye and left.

He was headed toward the gym when he heard someone calling him. Turning around he saw Bill Walters walking toward him. "Wait up and I'll walk with you," Bill said.

Walters was a member of the Victoria Junior College Track Team. An excellent sprinter, he participated in both the 100- and the 200-yard dashes. His family had recently moved to Edna and Bill was now in his second year at Victoria College.

Bill shook Victor's hand and said, "I hear you're going with us to the Texas Relays in Austin tomorrow."

"Yes, Coach Shinn asked me to come up today so we could leave early in the morning."

"Good. You can spend the night in my room."

They walked toward the gym where they were to meet Coach Shinn and the other members of the track team. Victor was excited about participating in his first track meet at the junior college level. He also looked forward to eating and spending his first night in a college dormitory. He was even beginning to be more certain about attending college. As he reflected on the events of that day, he kept remembering Florinda and the strong attraction he had felt toward her — a strange new feeling for him. Nor could he explain the reason for his feelings. But all in all, he surmised that he was pleased with his visit with the head of the art department to explore his future field of study.

The Sprint-Medley Relay

Friday, April 7, 1951, began slowly for four members of the Victoria College track team. Coach Shinn woke them up at six, and after a breakfast of bacon and eggs in the athletic cafeteria they left for Austin in two cars driven by the coach and one of the track team student managers. Bruce Miller, Bill Walters, Duane Mullenix, and Victor rode in the car driven by Shinn, while team manager Bill Yeager took the luggage and track equipment in the other car.

The Texas Relays were held on the University of Texas campus. It was, and still is, one of the greatest outdoor track meets in the nation. Athletes compete in four divisions from the university, college, junior college, and high school levels. The competition is intense and many world-class athletes have left their marks in these record books.

The Victoria Junior College Sprint-Medley Relay Team, on April 7, 1951, established a new Texas Relays record. From left, Bruce Miller, Duane Mullenix, Bill Walters, and Victor Rodriguez.

Knowing there would be tough competition was a challenge to Coach Shinn. This was only his second year of building a good track program at Victoria and it would be his first try at competing in a nationally-recognized meet. His team would compete in the freshman-junior college division in the sprint-medley relay, the four runners doing sprints of 440 yards, 220 yards, 220 yards, and 880 yards. Miller would take the lead-off 440 yards, Mullenix would run 220 and Walters the next 220, and Victor would take the final two laps which would cover 880 yards — the equivalent of a half mile.

Austin is about 180 miles from Victoria and the drive took three hours. The day started out with a clear sky and temperatures in the mid-seventies, but by the time they got to Austin the skies were overcast and there was thunder in the hills west of town. The members of the track team and Coach Shinn checked into the Stephen F. Austin Hotel just before noon. After a light lunch of roast beef, baked potato, dry toast, and tea, the boys changed into their running gear and sweat suits. The sprint-medley relay would take place at three o'clock.

They got to the stadium at one-thirty, just in time to witness the 5,000-meter run. By now the clouds overhead were nearly black, the thunder was loud, and streaks of lightning flashed across the sky. A few raindrops began to fall and a northerly wind cooled temperatures from the mid-seventies to the lower fifties. Suddenly there was a bright lightning flash and a loud blast of thunder, and the rain came down in sheets. The spectators, athletes, and meet officials scurried under the stadium, and the track was soon covered with two inches of water. The P.A. system announced a temporary postponement of the track meet. The heavy downpour continued for almost an hour, although to the athletes it seemed much longer. Athletes have a great deal of anxiety and nervous energy before any competition, and waiting for any length of time becomes nerve-wracking and frustrating.

Finally the rains ceased just as suddenly as they had begun, although the dark clouds still loomed overhead. The spectators, athletes, and officials returned to the stadium seats and it was announced that the running of the Texas Relays would continue according to the schedule except that all events would run one hour late. This meant the sprint-medley relay was postponed until four o'clock.

Although the rains had come down hard, the track had good drainage and the surface water had drained rapidly, leaving the black cinder track saturated but clear of any visible puddles. At 3:15, Coach Shinn told the team to begin their warm-up routine. The four boys trotted onto the football field and each went into his own routine of loosening up with slow jogging and stretching exercises.

This would be the first time that this foursome would compete together as a sprint-medley relay team. Bruce Miller was a powerfully built runner who excelled at the 440-yard run but he had never competed in a relay race of this kind. Duane Mullenix was a short, stocky fellow with better than average speed; he had run a 110-yard leg on the relay team but not a sprint-medley. Bill Walters was a champion 100-yard and 220-yard sprinter but he too hadn't competed in this sort of relay race. Victor was a distance runner who had excelled in the early cross-country season but he had not run a sprint-medley and he was to be the anchorman of the team! This was probably the least experienced team of the eight entered in the event, for they had never once practiced together handing off the baton from one runner to the next.

They went about their business of warming up in nearly total silence. Despite their inexperience, their quiet, serious manner showed a desire and commitment to win, and though they were nervous, they masked it from each other to keep up their confidence. At 3:55 the call came for all members of the sprint-medley relay teams to report to the starting line.

There were eight teams participating in this event. Texas University was in lane one, Texas A&M lane two, Oklahoma State lane three, Rice lane four, Kansas in lane five, Baylor lane six, Drake lane seven, and Victoria Junior College in lane eight. After they received their lane assignments, the runners were told to report to their assigned positions on the track where they would receive the baton from their teammates. When all were in place, the first runner from each team took his position at the starting line.

The starter raised his gun in the air and gave the command, "On your mark . . ." Everyone in the stands fell silent as the runners settled into their blocks. The starter gave his second command, "Get set . . ." The runners rose in their starting blocks to a four-point stance. The starter fired his gun and the runners shot out of their blocks and were off and running. This first 440 yards was one full lap around the oval track. Since Victoria's Miller was on the outside lane he had a staggered start ahead of the runners on the inside lanes. Bruce broke out around the first curve and into the backstretch, and while he was ahead of the runners in lanes one through seven, they had made up more than half of the staggered distance going around the first curve.

Approaching the end of the backstretch they headed into the second curve, and again the runners on the inside lanes made up some additional distance between them and Bruce Miller. As the runners approached the homestretch the second runner from each team positioned himself to receive the baton from the incoming runner at the end of the first full lap. Bruce Miller came in even with the runner to his inside as he handed off the baton to Duane Mullenix who took off as fast as he could go on his 220 yards. In the meantime, all the competitors on the inside lanes made up additional ground and passed Duane as they rounded the turn and entered the backstretch. Duane handed the baton to Bill Walters who took off full speed, still running in the eighth lane. At this point Victoria was running last but as they came off the curve and headed into the homestretch Bill accelerated and brought the team into fifth place.

Anchorman Victor waited for Bill in the eighth lane. Walters came in strong and handed over the baton. This was the 880 or half-mile stretch for two laps around the track, but these runners could break for the pole and run on the inside instead of staying in their assigned lanes. Victor took the baton from Bill and quickly but carefully negotiated his way from the outside to the inside lane next to the curb. As the anchormen entered the first turn of the first lap Victor could see four runners ahead of him. The lead runner, the anchorman for the University of Texas, was about thirty yards ahead. OSU was five yards behind Texas, chased by Kansas and Rice.

Victor decided if he was going to catch the runners ahead of him now was the best time to try. He made his move on the backstretch of the first lap. As they entered the second turn Victor was on the outside shoulder of the second-place runner, Oklahoma State. With a sudden burst of speed Victor spurted past him and was on the heels of the first-place runner. He pulled up even with the Texas runner, then accelerated and was leading the pack of anchormen as they approached the end of the first lap.

At the beginning of the final lap the starter fired his gun, which was the traditional signal to the spectators that this was the last lap. As they rounded the curve and headed into the backstretch, Victor was surprised at how easy it had been to overtake the other runners. Did they think he had over-paced himself? Were they conserving their energy and strength so they could overtake him in the backstretch? Around the last curve? In the final homestretch? He didn't know what their strategy might be so he concentrated on just running his own race.

Entering the end of the backstretch of the second lap, Victor's mind began its stream of advice. *"You're in the lead so don't worry about them,"* his mind said. *"Give it everything you have now that you have the lead. . . . They don't expect you to accelerate until you come into the home-stretch. If you accelerate in the middle of the last curve instead of waiting until you hit the final stretch you might surprise them and then it will be too late for them to catch you."*

He could feel the numbness in his legs as he entered the final curve. He tried to relax without losing any speed, but he knew that his mind was right, and as he entered the middle of the last curve he gritted his teeth and went into an all-out sprint. The spectators roared with approval as he hit the homestretch about 100 yards from the finish line. Another 50 yards and his legs were tightening up and he was finding it extremely difficult to breathe. He could tell from the reaction of the crowd that another runner was gaining on him fast. Resisting the temptation to look back, he kept his eyes focused on the finish line, and with all the strength he could muster he made a final lunge for the tape. As Victor broke the finish line tape, the runner from Oklahoma State fell to the ground at his right.

Victoria Junior College established a new Texas Relays record by covering the distance of the sprint-medley relay in 3 minutes 33.5 seconds. The four runners each received a gold medal for a first-place finish. They were also awarded gold miniature track shoes with a diamond in the toe for their record-breaking effort.

This triumph served as the catalyst that would propel Victoria Junior College to recognition as a national track power. It also brought recognition to its anchorman, Victor Rodriguez, who had come from behind and brought his team to victory against a strong field of freshmen teams from the Southwest Conference and the mid-west. Many of the track coaches from the senior colleges and universities made it their personal business to introduce themselves and congratulate Victor. Still others sent letters and notes congratulating him and extending invitations to consider attending their schools upon completion of his eligibility at Victoria Junior College.

Coach Eddie Shinn congratulated Victor with an affectionate hug and beamed as he said, "Vic, I'm so proud of you! You know that this is the first record we've set at the Texas Relays! Come to think of it, this is the first time we've ever *won* an event at the Texas Relays!"

Victor, still getting back his breath, just said, "Thank you." Overwhelmed by all this attention, he was self-conscious as he walked among the athletes and spectators with so many eyes focused on him, and he could hear comments as they referred to him as "that runner from Victoria."

The drive back to Victoria was very different from the trip to Austin. Going up they had been quiet, each suffering a certain amount of nervousness and anxiety. On the return trip, they were talkative and full of pride and relief. When they arrived in Victoria, the coach and athletes were in for another surprise. As they drove onto the campus, they saw a large banner covering the entrance to the gym with **WELCOME HOME CHAMPS** painted in 12-inch letters. The news of their victory beat them home.

Coach Shinn drove Victor to the bus station where he boarded a bus to Edna. Forty minutes later, he was walking briskly home, anxious to share the news with his mother and sisters. As he reached his own neighborhood, the dogs ran out one by one and greeted him as he walked in the middle of the street in the darkness of the night.

Jesus Gonzales

The neighborhood was very quiet and at first Victor thought maybe everyone had gone to bed early. Then he remembered this was Saturday night and everyone would be at the dance. He walked up on his porch, opened the screen door, and went to the kitchen where he found the kerosene lamp on the table. He took a match from the box, struck it, and lit the lamp. The yellowish light revealed a plate with two tacos wrapped neatly in brown paper from a paper bag. As he looked around the small kitchen he saw a clean change of clothes neatly folded on a chair. He pulled another chair out from under the small round table and sat down. He was about to unwrap the tacos when he heard footsteps on the porch, and Jesus Gonzales came through the door.

"Hey, Jesse!" Victor greeted him. "You're just in time. I was about to eat some tacos."

Jesus was quiet as he walked over and sat in a chair next to Victor. He had a bottle of beer in his left hand and he set it on the table. Victor unwrapped the tacos and offered one but Jesus pushed the plate away and said, "No, man, I'm not hungry." He took a big gulp from the bottle of beer and sat there, saying nothing.

"You sure you don't want a taco?"

Jesse still didn't speak, just gestured no with a wave of his hand while at the same time taking another gulp of beer. Something was obviously bothering Jesus. They had been friends since they were elementary students in the Mexican-American school so they knew each other's moods and temperaments well.

"*Que pasa?*" Victor asked, to encourage him to talk about what was

97

bothering him. Except for the time when Jesus' older brother Abelino had offered them a taste of beer to satisfy their curiosity, neither Victor nor Jesus were beer drinkers. Now, here was Jesus, drinking or rather gulping beer like a thirsty man drinking water.

Victor felt the warmth of the bacon, potato, and egg tacos and once again offered one to Jesus. The smell of the tacos was too much for Jesus, and he picked one up and took a big bite.

"*Que Padre*," (Great!) Jesus said and then asked, "You got any chilipin to go with this?" Chilipin is a sauce made from some very small red and green peppers just larger than buckshot. They are extremely hot. Victor's mother grew the small peppers, and he reached up and got a jar of her sauce from a shelf. Jesus took a spoonful of the hot sauce and spread it on his taco. He took a big bite and suddenly the sound of loud honking preceded the squeal of screeching brakes in front of the house. Victor ran outside and retrieved Jesus' bicycle which in his depressed mood he had left in the middle of the street. A pickup driven by an Anglo cowboy had barely missed running over the bike.

The angry cowboy yelled, "The reason you damn Meskins don't have anything is because you don't take care of what you have!" With that, he slammed his pickup in gear and burned rubber as he sped off into the night.

Victor put the bike by the porch and went back to the kitchen. He sat down in the chair next to Jesus who was resting his elbows on the kitchen table while holding his head with both hands. By this time, he had finished his taco and was halfway through the next one.

"Your mom makes great tacos," Jesus said and then asked, "How was your day in Austin?"

Victor heard the despondent tone of his friend's voice and knew his problem must be pretty serious to leave his bicycle in the middle of the street. Jesus' bicycle was probably his most prized possession and he had carelessly left it where some drunken gringo could run over it with his pickup. And there was the beer . . .

Victor was running through possible reasons for his friend's behavior. Did he steal something? Did he get in a fight and stab someone? Could he have gotten some girl pregnant?

Getting a girl pregnant was very serious, especially if you weren't willing to marry her. Not long ago one of their friends, Pio, had gotten a girl pregnant. Pio had been very reluctant to marry her until he received some very strong encouragement from the girl's male cousins who had "talked" to him. A month passed and Pio had still not married the girl, so one Saturday night the four cousins invited Pio to leave the dance and join them for a drink in their car. After having a couple of drinks, they took him for a little ride in the country. They drove around for a while drinking whiskey, then stopped on a secluded road and ordered Pio to get out. They pushed and rolled him down into an old irrigation ditch which ran parallel to the road and when he reached the bottom, the four pounced on him before he could get up. Two of them grabbed his arms and brought him to a sitting position while a third sat on his legs just below his knees. The fourth stood with a bottle of whiskey in his hand. He reminded Pio once again that since he had gotten the girl pregnant it was his obligation to marry her. He took a drink from the half-filled whiskey bottle and then passed it around to his brothers. After each took one more drink, they forced the rest of the whiskey into Pio's mouth, and when it was gone, the cousin who was standing broke the bottle in half on a rock. While the three held him down, the fourth man raked the jagged glass across Pio's right cheek, leaving a bloody, open cut that would scar him for the rest of his life. A week later Pio married the pregnant girl.

Victor knew that Jesus was one of the most honest individuals that he had ever known so he ruled out the possibility that Jesus had stolen something. He also knew that Jesus would not stab anyone unless his life depended on defending himself. And lastly, he knew that Jesus was too bashful to even ask a girl for a date. He didn't have a girlfriend. So what could be bothering him to cause this kind of change in his behavior?

"Are you going to tell me about your trip to Austin?" Jesus repeated his question.

Victor told Jesus about the victory in the Texas Relays and showed him the gold medal and the miniature track shoe with the diamond in the toe.

"Man, this is really something," said Jesus. "I'm really proud for you." It was almost midnight and Victor remembered that he had to go and walk his mother and sisters home from the dance.

"You want to go to the dance with me?" Victor asked. He thought maybe he could get Jesus to tell him his problem while walking to the dance.

"No, I'm a little bit tired. I think I'll just go home."

As they walked out on the porch, Jesus saw his bicycle and bent over and picked it up. "Thanks for taking care of my bike," he said as he reached out and firmly shook Victor's hand. He got on his bicycle and was about to leave when he stopped and said, "You're a good friend, and your mother makes good tacos. You go on to the dance and I'll talk with you mañana after church." He pedaled off into the darkness. Victor walked in the opposite direction and headed toward the dance to meet his mother and sisters.

* * *

On Sunday, April 9, 1951, the *Victoria Advocate* reported the record-breaking victory of the Victoria College foursome on the front page of the sports section. The picture of the four runners appeared with the following caption under the picture:

> Victor Rodriguez and Bill Walters of Edna, first and second from the right, are pictured above with their teammates at Victoria College. The quartet set a new Texas Relays Sprint-Medley relay record in Austin, April

7, running the one mile distance in 3:33.5. Rodriguez came from behind on the final 880 yard lap after Walters had run a 220 yard lap before him. Bruce Miller, left, ran 440 yards and was followed by Duane Mullenix, second from left, who ran 220 yards. Walters and Miller, along with Glenn Hoffman, not in the photo, are to take part in the National Junior College track and field meet in Kansas this weekend.

Victor was not aware of the picture and its caption that had appeared in the newspapers, but one of the Anglo residents of Edna had given a copy to Father Smiers. Before delivering his usual Sunday sermon, Father Smiers announced the newspaper story to the entire congregation.

"I am not surprised by his most recent success," he began. "Victor has been ringing the church bell every morning since he was in the third grade. Next month he will graduate from high school and he will have to decide whether or not to attend college." He asked the congregation to pray for Victor in order to help him arrive at his decision.

After mass, people came and shook Victor's hand as he stood with his mother and sisters. Jesus came over and asked Victor if he wanted to go down to the river and swim.

"Yes," said Victor. "Just let me go home and get out of my Sunday clothes."

He had hardly changed into his blue jeans and T-shirt when Jesus came riding up the street on his bicycle. They headed west toward the river, Victor sitting on the handlebars as Jesus pedaled the first mile before they changed positions and Victor pedaled the rest of the distance to the bridge. Leaving the bicycle under a tree, they walked up the river to their favorite swimming hole. They jumped into the water naked and swam around for a while, then Victor got out and put on his undershorts. As he lay there watching Jesus swim, he again admired his friend's ability in the water. He could still swim faster than anyone Victor had ever seen, even when going upstream against the strong current.

After a while Jesus came out and put on his undershorts and lay on the sandy riverbank beside Victor. The only sounds were the rushing river water and the chirping of birds in the trees.

Jesus was the first to break the silence. "Hey, man, I'm sorry I ate your taco last night. I just wasn't thinking straight. I came by to see you twice after I received the letter, but your mom told me you were in Austin."

"What letter?"

"The letter from the draft board. I didn't pass the examination to join the Army."

"I don't understand. You're in better shape than a lot of guys who served in the war."

Jesus looked sternly at Victor as he reached into his pants pocket and took out an envelope. He handed the letter to Victor and said, "Remember what I told you about staying in school?" The expression on his face grew even more serious and he went on, "During the war they would take anyone who could breathe and walk. Now they have other rules. The examination is not just physical any more. Now they test you for reading, writing, and spelling."

Victor took the letter and read it carefully. In disbelief, he read the final paragraph: ". . . We therefore regret to inform you that you do not meet all of the examination requirements necessary to qualify for entry into the U.S. Army."

"Why didn't you tell me about this last night?" asked Victor.

"After hearing of your good fortune in Austin, I didn't want to spoil your night," Jesus said. He put his hand on Victor's shoulder and said, "In another month, you'll graduate from high school. I know that you wanted to join the Army with me . . ." A broad smile crossed his face for the first time. "But since I can't go in the Army and take care of you I think you better forget about the Army and go on to college."

The Test

The month of May 1951 was a busy time for Victor. Because he was still a senior in high school he wasn't eligible to compete in the National Track and Field Championships in Hutchinson, Kansas, but he was well satisfied with his participation on the Victoria College track team and now he was looking forward to his last month of school. Everything was going well for him and he was seriously considering going on to college. All he had to do was make a passing grade in all of his subjects and then pass all his final exams.

He was doing fine in English, math, history, and physical education, but he was having a real problem with chemistry. His chemistry teacher was F. D. Ray, an excellent teacher as well as the principal of the high school. He only taught one course and that was the chemistry course which was required for all seniors. Victor knew that if he were going to graduate he would have to make a passing grade of at least 70 on his final chemistry exam. In his daily work and his lab performance he had a grade point average of 70, but he would still need at least 70 on the final.

Everybody in the class was aware of Victor's dilemma and they all offered to tutor him. Babe McDowell, who had graduated the year before by the skin of his teeth, advised him to memorize all the formulas on the wall chart in the chemistry room. Babe had been the quarterback on the football team the year before and he, along with several other athletes, had also had trouble with chemistry. Pat Davis, one of Victor's senior classmates, offered to help too. Davis was one of the smartest students in school and he happened to be in the same chemistry class with Victor.

Alfred Egg at the grocery store asked Victor how he was doing in school. "Are you passing all of your classes?" he asked one day as they were stocking the shelves.

"Yes," Victor replied, surprised that Mr. Egg was interested in his progress in school. "I'm doing fine in everything except chemistry."

"Who teaches chemistry?"

"Mr. Ray," answered Victor, a little embarrassed about admitting his shortcoming to his boss.

About this time James Miller, Mr. Egg's son-in-law, came over and joined the conversation. Miller was also the store manager and he had taken an interest in Victor's staying in school. He was also a great sports fan and kept up with Victor's participation in football and track. Everyone in Edna knew James Miller and for some reason that Victor never knew everyone called him "Doc."

Mr. Egg said, "Doc, Victor tells me he's having trouble passing chemistry in F. D. Ray's class,"

"Is that right?" Doc said, turning to Victor. "Well, don't worry about it, I'm sure you'll pass the final exam," he said as he walked away.

The more Victor thought about it though, the more he did worry about it. If he didn't pass he wouldn't graduate. If he didn't graduate he couldn't go to college next year. And then out of the clear blue sky an odd thought crossed his mind. If he didn't go to Victoria Junior College he might not see Florinda again! He decided to study hard and not think about failing, but try as he might, the thought of failure and its consequences haunted him day and night. Next week would be the last week of school and the final exam in chemistry would be on Tuesday.

*　*　*

The Saturday before the final week, Victor was bagging groceries in Mr. Egg's store when F. D. Ray walked in.

"Hello, Victor," Mr. Ray greeted him.

"Hello, Mr. Ray."

"Are you ready for next week?"

"I think so," Victor replied nervously.

Doc Miller and Mr. Egg came up and said hello to Mr. Ray. Mr. Egg said, "I sure would hate to see Victor not graduate just because he can't pass a damn chemistry test."

Victor was shocked and embarrassed and he wished he could just disappear.

Mr. Ray was about to say something more when Doc Miller spoke up. "We all think a lot of Victor and we sure would hate to see him fail chemistry. Besides, he's passing all his other subjects."

Mr. Ray stood there facing both men, and with a glance at Victor he told them, "Victor is a fine young man and I'm certain that with your interest and support, he will do all right. How much do I owe you for these groceries?" he asked as if to change the subject.

In the meantime, Victor stood frozen and terrified at what he had just heard. He was embarrassed for himself but he was even more embarrassed for Mr. Ray! He knew that Doc Miller and Mr. Egg had meant well, but he hadn't expected them to confront Mr. Ray about his personal situation.

The rest of the day, Victor tried to keep his mind on bagging and carrying out groceries, but as the day went by, other customers voiced their good wishes to him on his final exams next week. This only served to remind him of Tuesday. It seemed to Victor that the whole town knew about his predicament and it made him most uncomfortable.

After work he went home and bathed and changed into the clean clothes his mother had left on the kitchen chair. He ate the two tacos she had left on the table, then looked at the clock on the kitchen shelf and saw that it was 11:45 so he left for the dance to walk his mother and sisters home.

Due in large measure to his success in football and track, Victor was very popular everywhere he went in Edna. Because he rarely took part in social activities, his appearance always drew attention from the regulars. They knew that he worked every spare minute away from school or sports. The Mexican people had come to regard him as a role model and held the highest expectations for him. That evening when they greeted him at the dance they congratulated him on his upcoming graduation from high school, unconcerned about his personal problem with the chemistry exam.

"Congratulations!" they said. "We're proud of you!" they said. "We knew you could do it!" they added. All of their good wishes, along with the recent involvement of Doc Miller and Mr. Egg, only served to increase Victor's anxiety about next Tuesday.

Sunday and Monday were two of the longest days of his life. On Tuesday morning he woke to the sound of the steam locomotive train engine as it went through town at 4:00 a.m. Unable to sleep any longer, he got up and washed his face as he prepared for his daily run to ring the church bell. He lit the kerosene lamp and reviewed the chemistry formulas from the notes Pat Davis had shared with him. After his routine of ringing the church bell and serving as altar boy for the early mass, he went on to school even earlier than usual. When he arrived, Pat Davis was waiting for him.

"I thought we might have a chance to do a little reviewing before the test," Pat explained.

"Thanks, Pat," Victor said. He knew that the review was just for his benefit since Pat was one of the smartest students in school. As a matter of fact, Pat Davis was probably a genius when it came to academics. A small, frail, rosy-cheeked boy, he was at least a year or two younger than the other seniors. He didn't participate in athletics but he admired those who did. He was a special admirer of Victor, and he wanted with all his heart to help him pass this chemistry final exam.

The chemistry test was scheduled for second period. First period was his English final, and Victor was one of the first students to finish. He asked the teacher, "Mrs. Gus" Schiewitz, if he could spend his remaining time reviewing for his chemistry exam, and she gave him permission, but before he could start, a student came in and handed her a note.

"Victor, you are to report to the principal's office at the beginning of next period," Mrs. Gus told him.

"But I have my chemistry exam next period, " said Victor.

"Well, since Mr. Ray is the principal *and* your chemistry teacher, I'm sure he'll work things out," she said as she handed him the note.

When the bell rang, Victor hurried down the hall to the principal's office. Mr. Ray was waiting for him with three lady visitors.

"Come in, Victor," he said. "These three ladies are from the American Legion Citizens Medal Award. You are one of the five seniors that they are interviewing."

"But Mr. Ray, I have my chemistry final exam this period."

"Don't worry about it," Mr. Ray said. "You can take the chemistry exam after school today. I'll leave you with these ladies now and see you after school."

Mr. Ray left, closing the door behind him.

One of the ladies stepped forward and introduced herself. "I'm Mrs. Druschel and these two ladies are Mrs. Miller and Mrs. White," she said. "Why don't you sit down here, Victor."

Victor had seen these ladies in Mr. Egg's grocery store but this was the first time he had been formally introduced to them. He knew Mrs. Druschel was the wife of a prominent banker in town and the other two ladies were also wives of prominent men in the business community. All three were wearing big hats of fine woven straw with bright yellow ribbons above the brim. They wore beautiful dresses and high-heeled shoes, and their gloves went almost up to their elbows. The presence of the ladies filled the room with a fragrance of perfume and the clean odor of soap.

Victor sat there dressed in his blue jeans and short-sleeved, white starched shirt. He smiled at the three ladies and said, "I'm glad to meet you."

Mrs. Druschel was the spokesperson and she explained to Victor that each year the American Legion awarded a citizen medal to one graduating senior as selected by their committee of three representatives of the Legion. Then each of the ladies asked Victor questions about his extracurricular activities and the offices he held as a member of the senior class. Victor explained that he was the editor as well as the artist of the yearbook. He told them he was the sergeant at arms for his class, and described his role as a waiter in the cast of the senior play. In response to further questions, he assured them that he had never been in trouble with the law.

After the ladies had taken turns questioning him, Mrs. Druschel said that she had one final question, and she asked, "Can you describe a civic responsibility that you have performed for this community and tell us for how long you have performed that service?"

Victor thought for a moment and then he remembered the "civic responsibility" Miss Lindberg had assigned him in the third grade in the Mexican-American school. "Well, I ring the church bell at St. Agnes every morning and I have been doing it every day since I was in the third grade."

The three ladies glanced at each other and then Mrs. Druschel got up and said, "This concludes our interview. We've enjoyed visiting with you. Your principal will announce the result of our selection for the recipient of this award on the night of the graduation ceremonies."

Victor stood, shook hands with each of the ladies, and left the office. The bell rang as he stepped out into the hall and he went to his third-period history class. The rest of the day dragged by. Victor had looked forward to taking his chemistry exam during the second period and getting it over with, and now he had to wait until after school to take the test.

As soon as last period was over, he hurried down the hall to Mr. Ray's office where he found the principal busy talking to a parent and a student. When he saw Victor come into his outer office, Mr. Ray excused himself from his conference and came to the outer office where Victor was waiting. Handing him a folder, he said, "Here is your final exam in chemistry. Go down to the chemistry room and you can take the test there. When you finish just leave it on top of my desk in the chemistry room."

Victor went down the hall to the classroom, and as he walked past Mr. Ray's desk he couldn't help noticing a stack of exam papers in a neat pile in the middle of the desk. Lying next to them were answer sheets. Not wishing to be tempted, Victor went clear to the back of the room and sat at the last table. He opened the folder and was about to write his name in the upper right-hand corner of the paper when he looked up and his eyes focused on the wall chart which contained all of the formulas and symbols he had studied so hard to memorize. In the past, Mr. Ray had always covered up this chart with a lab apron when an exam was given. Did he forget to cover it up this time? Did he also forget the answer sheets on top of his desk? Victor was puzzled by this strange turn of events. He glanced down at his exam paper and saw that the first ten questions had to do with providing the symbols for ten elements. The other ten questions called for filling the blanks with the appropriate formulas. He knew that all he had to do to pass the test was to refer to the wall chart, but he decided to ignore it and to rely instead on his own memory and all those hours of cramming.

It took him about forty-five minutes to finish the test. He put it on top of the other exam papers on Mr. Ray's desk and walked out of the room. He was relieved that the test was over, and he was also glad he hadn't used the wall chart to help him answer the questions. He thought he had come up with the right answers from his own memory and that he had done all right. He walked past Mr. Ray's office and saw the principal was still there. When he glanced up and saw Victor standing there he motioned for him to come in.

"Well, did you do okay on the test?" Mr. Ray asked as he took off his eyeglasses.

"I think I did okay," Victor answered. "You forgot to cover up the wall chart."

"I completely forgot about the wall chart," Mr. Ray said. "Did you use it to pass the test?" he asked, looking Victor squarely in the eye.

Without blinking, Victor answered, "No sir, I relied on my own memory."

"Good. I'm glad you feel good about the test. I'll grade your paper in the morning and give you the results."

"Thanks, Mr. Ray. I'll be here bright and early."

The next day Victor woke up earlier than usual and went through his regular routine of ringing the church bell and went to school to sit on the front steps and wait for Mr. Ray. Pat Davis got there earlier than usual too and came to sit next to Victor.

"Morning," Pat greeted him..

"Morning, Pat."

The boys sat there in silence for a moment and then Pat said, "You don't have to worry about that chemistry exam — I know you passed it."

"How do you know that?"

"Oh, it's just a feeling I have."

About that time, Mr. Ray came out of the building. He said hello to the boys and said, "Come on in, Victor, and I'll give you your test results."

As Victor got up, Pat gave him a thumbs-up sign and winked at him. Mr. Ray unlocked his office door and invited Victor to come in and have a seat. There where three chickens lying on the floor next to the desk. Their legs were tied together with light cord and they wiggled and flapped as Mr. Ray walked around his desk.

"These three chickens were roaming in the hallway when the

custodian opened up the building this morning," Mr. Ray explained. "Some pranksters broke into the school last night and put these chickens in the hall."

Victor was more concerned about his exam results than about chickens. Mr. Ray opened his briefcase and took out a stack of papers. Victor could see that they were the chemistry exam papers. Mr. Ray handed Victor his paper and to his surprise and shock he saw a big 95 written in red at the top of his paper! He hadn't expected to make better than a passing grade of 70 on this exam, and a 95 was better than he could have dreamed!

He flipped through his test paper and Mr. Ray got up, came around his desk, and stood behind him. He put his hand on the boy's shoulder and asked, "Victor, are you certain that you did not refer to the wall chart in the chemistry room when you took this test?"

Victor turned in his chair and looked up into Mr. Ray's eyes and said, "No sir, I did not look at the wall chart, although I was tempted to several times."

"I was just curious, because you erased your answers several times, and the answers you changed to were the correct answers."

Victor sat there dumbfounded. As he looked at his paper, he could see that some of his original answers had been erased and changed. He didn't remember changing more than a couple, yet he could see clearly that at least a half-dozen more had been erased and changed!

"Well, Victor, I believe you are telling me the truth," said Mr. Ray, and he added as he shook Victor's hand, "Congratulations, it looks like you are going to graduate with the rest of your class."

Victor was happy to hear Mr. Ray's words but he was mystified at the high score he had made on the test. Moreover, he was curious about the number of answers that had been erased and changed. This was a mystery that would remain with him for years to come.

On graduation night all sixty-three seniors received their diplomas. It was the largest graduating class in the history of Edna High School. Besides the usual awards presented to the students graduating with the highest academic grade-point average, there were some special awards that night. Franklin Marek was the outstanding male athlete and Dorothy Denard was the outstanding female athlete. Bobbie McDowell and Victor Rodriguez were named the best all-around girl and boy. Victor Rodriguez was also given the American Legion Citizen Award Medal.

After the ceremonies were over, Victor joined his mother and sisters as they started to walk home. Mr. Ray came over and said hello to the Rodriguez family. As they were walking out of the auditorium Mr. Ray turned to face Victor and said, "I want you to know that I believe you passed your final chemistry test without referring to the wall chart. You will face many other tests in the years ahead. Only time will tell whether or not I was correct in believing you, but I have a great deal of trust and faith in you and I have no doubt that time will prove me right."

With that, Mr. Ray walked away as Victor and his mother and sisters began their way home.

The Edna High School Senior Class of 1951. Top: Miz Guz, Perry Campbell, Calvin Wilkerson, Weldon Bonnot. Second row: Dean Partridge, Jennie Clifton, Cleburn Belcher, Betty Davis, Louise Cornelius, Yvonne Crabb, Martha Miller, Lucille (Donons) Skoruppa, Margie Sklar, Geneva Greenawalt, Rose Marie Gabrysch, Mary Ellen Searcy, Joyce (Kennedy) Janak, Trois Marthiljohni, Blanche Goppert, Erlene Kubecka, Willie Mae Gates, Oretha Siecko, Pat Davis, Billy Porche. Third row: Bobbie Lou McDowell, Billy Elswick, Ruth Cavel, Howard Muscheck, Joan Randall, Wilma Tipton, Billie Jo Volkmer, Rita Griffith, Margie Cleveland, Patty Lou (Waters) Flourney, Jean Bennett, Geneva Grossman, Peggie Thomasson, Hazel Hunter, Betsy Baker, Helen Holstein, Edwin Goad. Fourth row: Jerry Cox, Tommy Tinker, Victor Rodriguez, Charles Sheblak, Jimmy Hessong, James Gandy; Billy Gene Yearwood, Clifford Wilkerson, Ellarein Gaubatz. Fifth row: Glen Whitely, Frances Minkert, Roger Melton, Jean Gerjcs, Lewis Watson, Dorothy Denard, Billie Nell Claybrook, Preston (Peanut) Miller. Not pictured are Carolyn Constant, Martha Gregory, Franklin Marek, Elsie Michalke, Ernest New, Chris Rosa, George Storz.

The Final Ringing of the Bell

The day following graduation night for the class of '51 marked the end of an era in Victor's life. This would be the last morning he would be performing his "individual civic responsibility" as the bell ringer for St. Agnes Church. Father Smiers had been forced to retire several years ago for old age and health reasons, and he was replaced by Father Buckley who accepted many of the traditional practices established by Father Smiers, including the responsibility that the church bell had to be rung each morning at 5:00 a.m. He was, however, relieved when Father Smiers explained that he need not worry about the ringing of the bell since Victor Rodriguez was taking care of this chore every morning.

Victor had already told Father Buckley this would be his last time to ring the bell. When he woke that morning he found it difficult to believe this was true. For nine years he had never failed to ring the bell except the few times he had been away on a trip with the track team. The ringing of the bell was such a daily routine that he had become almost oblivious to everything that happened on the route.

He left his house that morning at a slower pace, wanting to cherish each moment and each occurrence to preserve them in his memory bank. There had been drastic changes since he had started this chore as a third grader. Then he and his family had lived in a small house in the deep east side in the Black community. This morning as he stepped out the door of his home, they were living in the small cottage the Wells boys had built for them in back of the Wells' family home in the heart of the Anglo community. As he jogged in the middle of the street he was aware of the nice shoes he was wearing; as a third-grader he had begun his jaunt barefooted. A hundred yards down the street Fritz, the German shepherd, started barking at him. It was a friendly bark that was like a good morning greeting. In the past, Victor had simply patted Fritz on the head once or twice or had completely ignored him, but this morning he stopped and gave Fritz a warm hug and the dog responded by giving Victor several licks on his face with his big red tongue.

The barking of the German shepherd woke up some of the neighbors. As they turned on lights they also turned on their radios, and western music filled the previously quiet morning. Hank Williams was singing "Your Cheating Heart" on radios on both sides of the street.

Farther down the street, Red, the golden retriever, came running out to meet him and again Victor stopped to give the dog a big hug. The lights and the music came on in the house on the left side of the street and now Hank Williams was singing "Honky Tonk Man." The barking of Red and the blaring radio woke up other neighbors and Victor could hear Hanks' voice on their radios too. As he jogged on through the Anglo neighborhood other dogs came out to greet him, and Victor slowed his pace long enough to give each a hug and a parting pat on the back. He was likely bidding farewell to these dogs, some of whom he had known almost nine years. He realized he had been the neighborhood alarm clock each morning by causing the dogs to bark at him.

Now he left the Anglo neighborhood, approached the railroad tracks, and jogged easily as he neared the Mexican-American community. The dogs came out eagerly and he recognized each one by its size and color. Their barking woke up the people on both sides of the street and he could hear the ranchero songs coming from the homes with radios. One was a corrido called, *"Juan Charasciado."* As he continued through the Mexican-American community it seemed to him that all the houses in this neighborhood had their radios tuned to the same Mexican radio station. There were very few Mexican-American homes on the route to the church, for most of them lived in a concentrated area to the left of

115

the road Victor traveled each morning, but the barking of the dogs and the sounds of music carried into the other Mexican-American homes, and the lights and radios turned on in a chain reaction.

As he came closer to St. Agnes Church he slowed again. He was approaching the house where Adolph lived, the short squatty bulldog which had often surprised him in the early morning hours, and Victor had always been a little leery of him. But since this was his last day to ring the church bell and perhaps he would never see Adolph again, he wanted to make a special effort to part on friendly terms. He had never patted the bulldog before — they kept a good distance between them. Victor stopped jogging and began to walk cautiously. As he drew even with the front of the house he could see the bulldog hiding behind a car parked on the street.

Adolph had positioned himself behind the front tire on the left side of the car. He seemed surprised to see Victor walking instead of running. As he approached the front of the car, Victor bent down and called the dog by the name he had given him.

"Here, Adolph," Victor called as he stuck out his hand, palm up. "Here, Adolph." And much to his surprise, the bulldog came out from behind the tire with his stubby tail wagging behind him. As the dog reached his outstretched hand, Victor patted the wrinkled forehead and Adolph came closer and rubbed his body against Victor's leg. Victor responded by picking him up and cuddling him in his arms. Then realizing that he had to ring the church bell on time, he put Adolph down and began to jog up the street. Adolph followed him for about a block and then turned back toward his home.

Victor opened the front door to the church and pulled on the string hanging from the ceiling inside the church entrance. The string was attached to the electric light bulb that snapped on. Running up the stairs past the choir balcony, he climbed up the ladder to the bell tower and took hold of the rope and began pulling it down and releasing it in a rhythmic sequence as the bell above him rang out.

The first time he had rung this bell Father Smiers had had to tie a knot in the rope just a little above Victor's head, and he had enjoyed grabbing hold of the knot and pulling down on the rope. By keeping a tight hold as the rope went up and down, his feet would leave the ground on the upward ascent. Now the same knot was at the level of his chest and he could pull it easily and hang on without being lifted off his feet. He had developed a sequential rhythm that resulted in the bell giving off a one, one-two ring . . . bang . . . bong-bong . . . bang . . . bong-bong. Over the years he had learned to ring the bell in this sequence so that it produced ten single and double rings without his even having to count them. It was a process that was so much a part of him that he could perform it even on those mornings when he was half asleep.

On this particular morning he was especially conscious of the final two rings and he tugged a little extra hard on the rope. This caused the bell to give off a final sequence of three rings instead of the usual two long bongs. He wondered if anyone noticed the difference in the final rings. He opened the shutters in the bell tower where he stood about ten feet below the big bell, and he could see a few lights in the windows of some of the houses below.

This was one of the highest locations in the city. The only object taller was the water tower. He could see lights turning on in other houses. In the distance he could see the big clock on the courthouse tower. It was 5:00 in the morning. By now all of the dogs were awake and barking and every once in a while he heard the crowing of a rooster. As he stood there taking in the early morning sounds he vowed that he would forever recall this special moment which in the past he had taken for granted . . . or ignored altogether.

* * *

He was in the process of closing the shutters when he heard a voice calling him from below. Father Buckley was standing in the choir balcony below him.

"Is there something wrong with the bell?" he asked.

"No," replied Victor, remembering the extra tug he had given the rope. "The bell is working just fine," he added as he descended the ladder to join Father Buckley.

"Good morning, Victor," said Father Buckley. "I thought I detected a different bell sound this morning," he remarked as he looked curiously at Victor.

Victor smiled but said nothing as they went downstairs to put on their gowns for the early mass. As he put on his altar boy gown Victor wondered if anyone besides Father Buckley had heard the different sound of the bell that morning. It was, after all, the final performance of his individual civic responsibility as a bell ringer.

PART II
BECOMING A MAN
1951-1957

First Job after Graduation

Victor worked for the Texas Highway Department during the summer of 1951. The THD was in the process of surveying the land parallel to Highway 59 for some improvements. This was a two-lane highway with traffic flowing in both directions all the way from Laredo to Houston. Over time, the speed limits had been increased gradually from thirty miles an hour to more than fifty, and the two-lane highway had become increasingly dangerous for the faster cars produced after World War II. Money from the federal and state governments was made available to each county in Texas to improve the state's highway system.

Mrs. Gus Schiewitz, Victor's high school English teacher, was approached by John Slaughter, one of her former students who was now an engineer with the Texas Highway Department in Edna. Slaughter had been assigned the task of conducting a survey of the land parallel to Highway 59 for its possible expansion and improvement. In order to accomplish this he needed to hire a couple of young men to help him. He asked Mrs. Gus if she knew of any responsible young men who were willing to work hard that summer and she recommended Victor and promised to have him contact John Slaughter.

That evening she drove to Victor's house and gave him the name and address where he could contact Slaughter at the THD office in Edna, and the next day Victor went to Slaughter's office and was greeted and invited to come in and have a chair. Slaughter explained to Victor that this job would require someone who was willing to work hard.

"I've heard a lot of nice things about you," Slaughter began. "The fact that Mrs. Gus has recommended you is in itself a compliment you should be proud of. You'll be working as a member of a four-man crew which will consist of myself, my chainman, you, and one other man."

He described the responsibility of each of the four members of the survey crew. "I'll be the engineer in charge of the team," he explained. "I'll use my survey instruments to lay out the direction of the route for the new highway. My chainman, Mr. Starks, will be responsible for stretching a one-hundred-foot chain in the direction that I give him. You and another man will carry a sack of two-foot-long stakes which are to be driven in the ground with a sledge hammer at the end of the one-hundred-foot chain. You or the other stakeman will drive a stake at the end of the chain every time it is stretched to the end. This will require a lot of stamina since we'll be surveying several miles a day." Slaughter's serious tone was intended to emphasize a commitment to working hard all day. He asked Victor if he had any questions thus far.

Victor thought for a moment and then asked, "Do you know who the other stakeman will be?"

"No, I'm still interviewing several men to find someone who's not afraid of a little hard work." He handed Victor some papers to fill out and said, "If you are interested in the job, it's yours. Just fill out these papers and report here next Monday morning." Then he added, "You should get yourself a cap or a good straw hat along with some gloves and a pair of old army combat boots. We'll be surveying some virgin land and you need to be dressed comfortably in order to survive a hard days' work."

Victor thanked Mr. Slaughter and assured him that he was not afraid of hard work. "I already have gloves, a straw hat, and a pair of army boots," he said as he was about to leave. "I used them when I was putting in fence posts on Mr. Egg's ranch." This seemed to reassure Mr. Slaughter somewhat.

"When you finish filling out the papers, just leave them with the secretary at the front desk," Slaughter said. "I'll see you here Monday morning at seven-thirty."

Victor left the Highway Department office feeling excited about the prospect of his job as a member of the survey crew and wondering who the fourth member of the crew would be. Slaughter had made commitment to hard work a requirement, but Victor had no concern about his own ability to be a good stakeman. There had been his years as the bell ringer and as an employee for Mr. Egg, plus mowing yards with a push mower, and cleaning out and preparing flower beds on Fridays and Mondays for neighbors of the Wells family. Everyone who knew him had always praised him for being a good hard worker.

He had always worked four days a week on Fridays, Saturdays, Sundays, and Mondays during the school year until he became a freshman in high school. When he earned a berth as a starting tackle on the football team that first year, he became known to everyone in Edna, and this resulted in people not hiring him to do work for them on Fridays and Mondays. They kept insisting that he should be in school.

"Does Manuela know that you're not in school?" they would ask. They would offer to hire him on Saturdays or Sundays, but one by one they all refused to hire him on Fridays and Mondays. It was as though the entire Edna community was committed to making certain that he go to school on Fridays and Mondays.

With his reputation as a hard worker, sometimes the praise for a job well done was almost as gratifying as the money paid him. He had grown up and matured faster than many young men his age. He had established a strong personal work ethic characterized by punctuality, reliability, honesty, and a commitment to hard work. It was these same characteristics which carried over in his success in football and track. And football and track had taught him a great deal about cooperation and teamwork. As a member of the survey crew, Victor felt very confident that he could measure up to being a good stakeman. He hoped that the other stakeman would share his same kind of commitment.

On Monday, Victor woke up at 4:15, his usual habit, then suddenly he remembered he was no longer responsible for ringing the church bell, so he lay back in bed enjoying a luxury he had seldom experienced in the past nine years. It would be three hours before he had to report to work that morning with the Texas Highway Department. As he lay in his bed wide awake, he heard the crowing of a rooster in the distance, and he wondered whether Father Buckley would be ringing the church bell that morning or had found someone else for the job.

Sometime while he was in high school, the Mexican-American school had ceased to exist. Although he couldn't recall the year, he knew it must have been between 1948 and 1951. He wondered where Lucille Lindberg might be. Without Miss Lindberg, there would be no one to assign a student to ring the church bell.

His thoughts were soon interrupted by the tone of a bell ringing. As he listened carefully he realized it was just the clock in the courthouse dome giving off a gong-like sound. It bonged five times indicating that it was five o'clock in the morning. There had been no sound of dogs barking, nor had the church bell rung at exactly five a.m. Victor got out of bed, dressed, and went into the kitchen. He was about to light the kerosene lamp when his mother came in. She too had heard the bonging of the courthouse clock at five. Victor looked at the only clock in the house, which was on top of the refrigerator. It was six minutes past five! The church bell had not been rung! His mother was about to say something when they both heard the church bell.

"Whoever is ringing the church bell is ringing it a little too late," Manuela said. "What time are you supposed to be at work?"

"At 7:30," Victor replied. "If I leave here at seven I can be there by 7:20."

"Since this is your first day, leave here at 6:45 and be there at 7:15 or a little earlier. That way you can insure being on time without the worry of being late. It is important that you make a good impression with your boss on the first day of work."

Manuela made a pot of coffee and took some dough out of the icebox. She had prepared the flour dough the night before. She rolled some pieces into four balls and flattened them out, one by one, using her wooden roller to spread each ball into a round tortilla. Since Victor had been the first member of the family to rise that morning, he had lit the wood in the iron stove and it was now just the right temperature to cook the tortillas.

"Thank you for lighting the stove, *mijo* (son)," she said as she placed tortillas on each of the four round, flat, removable covers on top of the stove. By the time the tortillas had been flopped over a couple of times the coffee was ready, and they sat down, buttered the tortillas, and enjoyed them with a cup of coffee. This was the first time in nine years that Victor had had the luxury of sitting down for breakfast and enjoying an early morning conversation with his mother. Father Smiers had some- times offered him a piece of buttered toast and a cup of coffee after the early morning mass but as he sat there with his mother, munching on his buttered tortillas, he was convinced again that she made the best tortillas in the world.

The time went by fast, and one by one Victor's sisters joined him and his mother in the kitchen. Theresa and Adela came in first, then Frances, the youngest, came and sat down after everyone else was almost through eating. Rafaela, the oldest girl, was in San Angelo where she had become a nurse.

Victor glanced at the clock on top of the refrigerator. It was 6:15. He grabbed his straw hat and tucked the old soft cowhide leather gloves in his back pocket and started out the front door. As he was about to step down from the small porch, his mother came to the front door and said, "*Adios, mijo, y buena suerte* (and good luck)." Her words always had a reassuring effect on Victor.

He turned and said, "*Gracias, Mama,*" and started walking toward the Highway Department office.

* * *

When Victor got to the Texas Highway Department office he was surprised to find no one else there. He walked around the building thinking someone might be parked in back of the building, but soon realized that he was the only person on the entire premises. He walked back to the front and sat down on the steps leading to the main entrance. The courthouse clock sounded its gong seven times.

Sheriff Watson drove by and waved at him. A few minutes later a second car drove up and stopped in the street. Someone got out on the passenger side, and the driver waved at Victor and drove on. Victor didn't immediately recognize the young man coming up the sidewalk dressed in blue jeans and combat boots and a straw hat. There was something familiar about his walk but it wasn't until he spoke that Victor recognized Bill Walters, his teammate on the track team at Victoria College.

"Hey, hombre," Bill greeted Victor in a surprised tone.

"Hi, Bill," Victor said as he moved over and gestured for Bill to sit down. "What are you doing here?"

"I'm here to work with John Slaughter as a member of a chain gang," Bill answered. "What about you?"

"Same thing."

"Well, I'll be darned."

"Small world, isn't it."

Although Victor and Bill had been on the winning track team together, they knew very little about each other beyond sharing in that common moment of glory. There was mutual admiration for their accomplishments on the track, but basically Victor regarded Bill as just another "gringo." This term was a reflection of Victor's growing up in Edna. As the only Mexican-American on the Edna Cowboy football team, Victor had associated with many Anglos whom he admired and respected, but there was never any mingling on a social level. It was through his accomplishments in athletics that he had been granted many rights and privileges not generally extended to local Hispanics. Victor was permitted to eat in the restaurants that had always denied service to Mexican-Americans, while even those who had come home wearing their military uniforms during World War II had not been served in Edna's cafes.

Victor's appreciation of these privileges was lessened by the fact that they weren't extended to other Mexican-Americans. The ethnic separation was simply accepted as a traditional way of life. Perhaps it was this "way of life" acceptance that prevented Victor, who was very popular in Edna — especially among his classmates — from accepting some of the opportunities to socialize outside of school activities. Some of the Anglo girls in school would sit with Victor in the library or in the cafeteria or school assemblies, but he would never accept their invitations to go to a dance or a movie. He just courteously declined and said he already had another date.

In contrast to Victor's relationship with his lifelong Anglo friends and their mutually shared "way of life", Victor had known Bill for little less than a year. During the 1950-1951 school year, Victor had been a high school senior while Bill was a junior college sophomore. As they sat there on the steps, Victor realized this was the first time he and Bill had ever had an exchange of conversation other than when they had traveled to and from track meets.

"When the summer is over, I'm going to North Texas State on a track scholarship," Bill said in a friendly tone. "What are you going to do, Victor? I understand that you have several scholarship offers."

"I do have several offers from colleges and universities, but I'd rather stay in Texas. Coach Shinn has been awfully good to me and I may just stay and run for him."

Bill was about to say something when they saw a yellow pickup pulling up with a State of Texas emblem on its door and big black letters reading "Texas Highway Department." The pickup came to a stop and

John Slaughter got out and came toward them. "Good morning. You ready to go to work?"

"We're ready," Bill answered, and Victor said, "Good morning."

"Well, let's go," said Slaughter, gesturing for them to get in the pickup. Bill and Victor walked around to the passenger side and Victor opened the door and said, "After you," as he politely stepped aside and motioned for Bill to get in and sit in the middle. Bill hesitated for a minute and looked ready to argue the point of who should sit where but when Slaughter gave them a stern look and said, "Come on, let's get going," Bill got in first and sat in the middle. Victor jumped in and sat on the side next to the door.

Although Bill didn't say anything, Victor could sense that he did not appreciate having to sit in the middle. On the other hand, Victor had a feeling that somehow he had won the first confrontation, small as it might seem, with Bill. He didn't suspect that this was only the first of many occasions when this kind of subtle, sometimes silent, competition would manifest itself between Bill and him in the summer months that followed.

During June, July, and August, the two boys worked hard driving stakes along Highway 59 between Edna and Victoria which would eventually become a four-lane expressway. The other task involved the widening and building of bridges to span three of the rivers and creeks along the same route. During this phase Victor and Bill were responsible for making certain that the proper ingredients of sand, gravel, and cement were mixed to produce the pylons that would support the bridge. It was their task to keep count of the number of sacks of cement that were emptied into the mixing machines. They each had a pocket-sized tablet where they recorded a stroke or stick figure each time a cement sack was emptied into the mixer. During their lunch breaks, which occurred at irregular times, they would occasionally have time for themselves under a shade tree along the river banks.

One day as they were sitting down to enjoy their brown bag lunches, Bill watched as Victor took something out of his lunch bag that was different from his own homemade sandwich.

"What's that you have there?" Bill asked.

Victor didn't know how to interpret Bill's question. Was he really curious or was he poking fun at him? He decided to give Bill the benefit of the doubt and accept the question as sincere curiosity. Like many of the Anglos he knew, Victor reasoned that maybe Bill wasn't acquainted with Mexican-American cuisine. Victor held up a taco and said, "That's a taco."

"A taco?"

"Yes, a taco," Victor replied, beginning to sound a bit defensive.

"What kind of taco?"

By now, Victor was becoming a little impatient. The subtle competitiveness in him was aroused and he said in a firm voice, "That is a bacon and egg taco with homemade salsa, wrapped in a tortilla made as only my mother can make them." And just in case Bill should be poking fun at him, Victor added, "This is what *real* men eat."

The emphasis on *real* men got Bill's attention as he considered Victor's response unnecessarily sarcastic. Bill was not about to let Victor have the upper hand in this harmless competitive dialogue, so he reached in his brown bag and pulled out a sandwich and said, "Well, this is a ham and cheese sandwich with lettuce, pickle, and tomatoes between two slices of delicious Buttercrust bread. This is an all-American sandwich."

* * *

During the ensuing months, the two young men continued this harmless kind of friendly yet competitive dialogue with each trying to outdo or outlast the other. Each seemed to get a certain kind of pleasure from these kinds of exchanges, but as they got to know each other, their conversations sometimes grew more genuine and sincere — especially when their conversations and discussions dealt with their futures in track.

Once during their lunch break, Bill mentioned again that he would be enrolling at North Texas State in the fall.

"Gosh," said Victor, "that's over three hundred miles away! Why are you going there?"

"It's a great school," Bill said. "They are the fourth largest college in Texas, and besides, they have a great track team."

Victor remembered seeing members of the North Texas track team at the Border Olympics and the Texas Relays. He had been impressed as they ran out on the field dressed in their silvery-white, hooded warm-ups which gave them a ghostly look. They stood out among the throngs of athletes, not just for their spectral appearance but by their succeeding performances. They had great sprinters and outstanding distance runners.

"So you're going to Victoria College," Bill said. "You should come to North Texas after you finish there."

Victor was pleased at this comment and felt obliged to respond with some equally favorable remarks. "We'll miss you at Victoria next year," he said with as friendly a tone as he could make it.

*   *   *

The summer continued to pass at a rapid pace and the chain crew did yeoman service in meeting their time schedule surveying and staking out the expansion of Highway 59. Perhaps it was the busy schedule which siphoned off some of the competitiveness between Bill and Victor. Or maybe it was just that they gradually got to know and understand each other.

Everything went very well until one Friday at quitting time. The members of the chain crew had put in a hard day's work and were completely exhausted after ten long hours under an unmerciful sun with the temperature at 100 degrees. Mr. Starks drove off in his own pickup. John Slaughter got in the other pickup behind the steering wheel and waited for Bill and Victor. Once again, Victor opened the door and said, "After you, Bill."

Bill was tempted to say something, but with Slaughter waiting and watching he reluctantly got in and sat in the middle once more. Victor jumped in and took his usual position next to the door. As they were headed home towards Edna, Bill couldn't help but notice the smirk on Victor's face.

"I only got in because we were in a hurry to get going — so wipe that smirk off your face," said Bill.

"If you hadn't gotten in, I would have thrown you in."

"No way," Bill quickly retorted and then having taken up the challenge said, "If this pickup were to stop, I would throw you down in that ditch."

John Slaughter was a quiet, serious-minded, hard-nosed man. He had endured the on-going friendly competitive challenges between these two all summer long. Suddenly without uttering a word, he pulled the pickup off the highway and parked on the right shoulder on top of a six-foot embankment. He shut off the engine, turned, and gave both boys the kind of stern look which only he could muster. Without a word, Victor and Bill got out of the pickup and faced each other squarely.

A grappling, shoving, and pushing match ensued. Although the details of what happened are not clear in Victor's mind, he wound up tumbling down the embankment into the ditch below. Perhaps his pride and ego caused his memory of that incident to blur.

The honking of the horn brought the boys back to the pickup. Bill opened the door and said, "After you, Victor."

Victor got in and sat in the middle. They drove on in silence until

Slaughter pulled the pickup to a stop in front of Victor's house. Bill got out first and allowed Victor to get out. Without saying a word, Victor walked up the stairs to the porch in front of his house. He was about to open the screen door when Bill, still standing by the pickup, called out to him, "Hey hombre, I'll see you Monday."

Victor turned slowly to look at Bill, and a broad smile crossed his face as he said, "If you're lucky." Slaughter could only shake his head as Bill got in the pickup and they drove off.

* * *

The summer was finally over. John Slaughter thanked Bill and Victor as he handed them their final paychecks. "I sure hate to see you two go," he said as he shook hands with them. Then he smiled and said, "You two will do well in college." He was about to leave, then turned back and added, "You are definitely two of a kind."

Bill enrolled at North Texas State in the fall of 1951 and Victor enrolled at Victoria Junior College. After being together and working hard that hot summer, they were now going their separate ways, at least for awhile, but they would continue their relationship in the years ahead — a relationship that would finally develop into a lasting friendship.

Freshman

It was the middle of September in 1951 when Victor walked into the only existing dormitory on the Victoria Junior College campus. This was the dorm which housed all the athletes involved in football, basketball, and track. The two-story building had a small lobby in the middle of the first floor, connected to two hallways running east and west. The cafeteria was on the north side and there was a stairway from the lobby to the second floor. As he stepped into the lobby Victor saw a man wearing a suit and tie sitting at a table with a young man and a young woman.

The man looked up and saw Victor, got up and came forward, and said, "Good morning, I'm John Stormont. I'm the dean and registrar for the college."

"I'm . . ." Victor started to introduce himself but Dr. Stormont interrupted him. "I know who you are, Victor, and I've heard a lot of good things about you. Come over here and meet my two assistants. They'll register you and assign you a room and roommate."

Victor shook hands with the two students as he read their names on the tags they were wearing. After he filled out a card with his name and home address, the young lady gave him a card with a room number on it. The young man told him, "Your room is located on the first floor and if you go down this hall, it will be the second door on the right."

Victor picked up the suitcase and a cardboard box which contained his clothing and other possessions and started toward his room. As he walked down the hallway he noticed a folding canvas army cot against the corridor wall. He opened the door to his assigned room and walked in. A young man was lying on the bed on the left side of the room.

He got up when he saw Victor and said, "You must be Victor Rodriguez. I understand we're going to be roommates. I'm Ramond Velasquez."

They shook hands and as a result of the old habit he often used when he couldn't think of anything else to say, Victor asked, "Where you from, Ramond?"

"Calvert."

Seeing that Ramond had taken the bed on the left side, Victor set his suitcase and box on the bed on the right.

"I took the closet on the left," Ramond said. "The closet on the right is empty."

Victor unpacked as he and Ramond exchanged small talk to get better acquainted.

*   *   *

The day went by rather fast and later Tommy Tinker came in the room. Tommy had been one of Victor's teammates on the Edna football team. He had graduated from high school with Victor and was attending Victoria on a football scholarship.

Tommy and Victor exchanged greetings and Victor introduced him to Ramond.

"I thought you might like to know it's time to eat dinner," Tommy said.

"Let's go!" said Ramond as he slipped on his shoes and left them unlaced. The three of them walked down the hall toward the lobby and the cafeteria. Victor noticed the army cot again, and saw that someone had put a suitcase and a small cardboard box on top of it.

The cafeteria was bustling with laughter, chatter, and the sound of knives and forks making contact with plates. The tables were rectangular with chairs for six people and many were already full. Tommy spotted a table with only three athletes and gestured for Ramond and Victor to follow him. Victor recognized two of the men seated at the table — Franklin Marek, an Edna teammate from their high school football team, and Glen Hoffman, a teammate from last year's Victoria track team. The third man was introduced to Victor as Inocensio Cantu, a freshman distance runner.

After the introductions, they sat down and helped themselves to dinner, which was served family style. During the conversation, Inocensio Cantu asked them to please call him "Ino." He said he realized they had difficulty pronouncing his name, so "Ino" was what they should call him. Ino was from El Campo, a small town east of Edna. Victor was quick to recall that Edna and El Campo were great football rivals.

After dinner they chatted for a while until the cafeteria workers started clearing and cleaning the tables. Tommy Tinker said he was going up to his room which was on the second floor. Franklin stopped in the lobby and said he was going to call one of his girlfriends.

Victor and Ramond were walking toward their room when Victor turned to Ino and said, "Why don't you come over and visit in our room for a while?"

"Okay," Ino replied and then asked, "May I come use your bathroom first?"

"Sure," said Victor, and Ramond added, "Come on in." They assumed that perhaps Ino had a room upstairs and didn't want to have to go upstairs first. As they were about to enter Victor's and Ramond's room, Ino stopped at the army cot in the hallway. He opened his suitcase and removed a towel, a bar of soap, and his pajamas.

Victor and Ramond asked almost in unison, "Is this your bed?"

Ino explained that all of the rooms were full and there were no vacancies left in the dormitory. He had been told that he would sleep in the hall temporarily until a janitor supply closet could be cleared out. Then he would be sleeping in the closet vacated by the janitor. In the meantime, he was told by Mr. Stormont that he could make arrangements to use the bathroom facilities of some of the other tenants. While Ino was showering, Victor and Ramond decided upon a solution to the problem. They moved their respective beds to the extreme right and left sides, thereby leaving enough space in the middle to accommodate Ino's army cot.

When Ino came out of the shower, he saw the room had been rearranged and his cot was in the middle between the beds.

"We decided to adopt you," Victor told a surprised Ino.

"That's right," said Ramond, with a broad smile.

"Gosh," said Cantu, "I hope I'm not crowding you guys." He was obviously pleased by the invitation to become their roommate.

The next morning, Victor, Ino, and Ramond had breakfast and went to the administration building to register for their fall semester courses. While they waited in line, Victor looked up from his hand-written schedule just in time to get a glimpse of Florinda Reyes who was standing in line on the far side of the room. Victor waved at her and she smiled and waved back. He was hoping he might see her later, but the day passed and he didn't see her again that day.

* * *

That fall the Victoria Junior College cross-country team participated in several meets against teams from the Southwest Conference. Despite the loss of such outstanding track performers as Bill Walters and Bruce Miller from the 1951 team, it looked like Coach Shinn was going to have another strong squad. On November 7, the Victoria Pirates defeated the A&M freshmen harriers at College Station. Ino Cantu finished first and Victor finished third over a 2.9 mile course. Cantu was a very pleasant surprise to Eddie Shinn who had recruited him on a half track scholarship. Victor found that he could easily beat Ino in the half-mile run in their practice workouts, but when it came to any distance over a mile Ino could always beat him.

Cantu was about five feet ten inches tall and could run all day at a slow steady pace. In Austin on November 14th, Ino set a record of 13 minutes and 33 seconds over a 2.8 mile course against the Texas University Longhorn Varsity. Victor finished fifth. In team scoring, however, the Pirates finished second to the winning Longhorn team. Three weeks later, in Victoria, the Pirates defeated the University of Texas Varsity, the ineligible squad, and the Texas freshmen over a 2.5 mile course. The final cross-country meet of the fall season was the Bill Williams A.A.U. in Houston. The Pirates took a second-place finish behind the A&M Varsity. Cantu finished fourth and Victor finished sixth behind some of the state's varsity performers from Texas A&M and North Texas State's only two entrants. The only freshman to finish ahead of Ino and Victor was North Texas' outstanding performer, Dale Imel. With the final meet of cross-country over, the track team looked forward to the track meets in the spring.

In between their training stints, Victor and Ino concentrated on their studies. Occasionally they would visit with Flo Reyes in the Student Union Building. Florinda had decided to form a Spanish Club on campus and she persuaded Miss Mary Doughtie, an English teacher, to sponsor it. She also talked Ino, Ramond, and Victor into voting for her to be the president of the club.

"If you vote for me to be president, you can become members of the club," she told them. They voted and solicited other students to vote for her, and she thus became the first president of the first Spanish Club at Victoria College.

On one of their visits with Flo, she seemed rather quiet and had little to say. Later in the afternoon Victor learned that one of Flo's brothers, Carlos Reyes, had been killed in a plane crash. Carlos was in the Air Force and was a trainer for beginning pilots. Upon learning the sad news, Victor

The Spanish Club at Victoria College. Founder and president Florinda Reyes is seated at center. Standing in back row, Victor Rodriguez at left, and Ino Cantu standing behind Florinda. Seated at their regular meeting are Cora Nell Browning, Dorothy Franz, Nicolasa Villafranca, Florinda Reyes, Tavita Hernandez, Carolyn Martin, Joyce Nixon. Standing are Dolores Tyng, Lillie Ramirez, Mary Gonzales, Helen Machost, Pauline Montier Cook, Victor Rodriquez, Robert Haring, Ynocensio Cantu, Betty Dick, Pat Sunkel, Tommy La Noue, Richard Greene, and Mrs. Mary Doughtie.

took the shuttle bus downtown and walked the remaining distance to Flo's boarding house. He knocked on the door.

"Is Flo here?" he asked.

"Yes," replied Mrs. Mayorga. "Come in." She motioned for Victor to step into the living room, then went down the hall, and he could hear her as she knocked on a door.

"Flo, there's a young man here to see you," Mrs. Mayorga said.

In a moment Flo walked into the living room and was surprised to see Victor. She invited him to sit down, and she sat on a sofa. Victor sat on the same sofa, but about two feet from her. After expressing his sympathy, he sat there quietly, not knowing what else to say.

Flo, noticing his shy manner, said, "I really appreciate you coming over."

Without thinking, Victor reached in his jacket pocket and pulled out a small jewelry box which contained a gold track shoe with a diamond in the toe. The shoe was attached to a gold chain. Victor handed the small box to Flo. She opened it and said, "Victor this is beautiful."

He was pleased that the shoe had caused her face to light up.

"Where did you get this?" Flo asked.

Victor explained how it had come to be awarded to him.

"I'm glad you showed it to me," said Flo. She put it back in the small box and handed it to him. Victor was glad that he had shared the history of the shoe with her. He was also happy that it had, at least for a moment, made her forget the sad news about her brother's death.

"I would be honored if you would wear it," Victor heard himself saying shyly.

"Thank you," said Flo as she reached behind her neck and snapped it on. "I'll wear it and keep it for you so you won't lose it."

Mrs. Mayorga walked into the living room and told Flo that she was wanted on the phone.

Victor said, "I guess I'll be going."

"Thanks for coming over and for the track shoe," Flo said as she walked to the door with him.

"I'll see you around the campus," Victor said as he turned and left.

* * *

During the spring the track team participated in several track meets. The first was the major national outdoor track meet known as the Border Olympics, held in Laredo. Participants included teams from all over Texas in the high school division as well as teams from Texas, New Mexico, Oklahoma, and Louisiana in the junior college, college, and university divisions. It was a two-day meet with preliminaries on Friday and finals on Saturday. In the university division, Oklahoma A&M won first place; in the college division, North Texas State was the champ, and Victoria Junior College led the junior college division. Ino Cantu won the mile run, and Victor won the half-mile run and ran a leg on the winning mile relay team. The following weekend the Victoria Pirates won their junior college division at the Fort Worth Southwestern Track Meet, with Victor and Ino once again victorious in their respective races.

The first week in April was the running of the Texas Relays in Austin. While the previous year Victoria had finished first in record-setting time in the sprint-medley, this year they finished third behind Oklahoma A&M and the University of Texas. Victor was learning a great deal about what it was like to compete beyond the high school level. Perhaps it was this loss that helped the members of the Victoria track team be better prepared mentally for their journey to Hutchinson, Kansas, to compete in the National Junior College Championships.

The first day of their journey to Kansas, the track team stopped in Denton and worked out on the North Texas track facility. They spent the night there and got acquainted with some of the track athletes from North Texas State. The following morning they had breakfast in the athletic dining room and continued on their way to Kansas. The track team arrived in Hutchinson on Friday around mid-afternoon. The sprinters and field events men competed in preliminary trials that night. Since there were no preliminaries in the distance races, Victor and Ino were automatically advanced into the finals.

The evening of the Saturday finals brought some steady showers for about an hour, then a light foglike mist that would continue throughout the night. The first running event of the evening was the one-mile run. Ino finished first and Victor, who had not run a mile race all year, finished fourth. Ino scored ten points for his winning effort and Victor earned four points for his fourth-place finish. The fourteen points they scored put Victoria College in the team lead after the first event of the night. This seemed to give the entire team an emotional lift which not only helped them maintain the lead but they opened up a gap that the other teams simply couldn't match.

Victor returned forty minutes later and scored another ten points with a first-place finish in the next to last event and won first place in the half-mile run in the final event. He also ran the third leg on the winning mile relay. When the final results were counted, Victoria Junior College had scored over 100 points, well ahead of the second place team with a total of 52 points. But of more importance was the fact that the Victoria Pirates had won their first National Championship.

On the trip back to Texas, the team stopped in Denton again to spend the night. Winton E. "Pop" Noah, the North Texas track coach, sought out Victor that evening and offered him a full scholarship in track for the following three years. Victor accepted Pop's offer as he knew that North Texas had an excellent team. Victor had been the first Hispanic athlete at Victoria since he had participated there while he was still a senior in high school. Ino and Ramond joined him as freshmen the following year. Now he would be the first Hispanic athlete at North Texas. And he would once again be a teammate with his old friend Bill Walters.

Upon the track team's return to Victoria, they were given many dinners and banquets in appreciation for bringing home a first National Championship.

*   *   *

This freshman year had produced memorable learning experiences for Victor, and he had made some lifelong friends. Ramond Velasquez had not only been a good roommate, but he earned a letter as an outstanding football player. Ino Cantu had also been an excellent "adopted" roommate and he had become a premier cross-country runner as well as a national champion in the mile and two-mile runs. Victor had won a national championship in the half-mile run.

Next year, Ino and Ramond would be returning to Victoria Junior College. Flo Reyes had told Victor that she would be transferring to Southwest Texas State. While Victor looked forward to next year when he would be at North Texas, he couldn't help but wonder if he would ever cross paths again with some of his fellow freshmen friends with whom he had shared such a memorable year.

141

Working on the Railroad

In June of 1952, Victor and his mother, along with Frances, the youngest of his four sisters (who had acquired the nickname of "Pat"), moved to San Antonio. Teresa had married and was living in Edna. Adela was working in San Antonio, and Rafaela, the oldest daughter, had married and also lived in San Antonio. Although Victor had some reservations about moving, he was convinced that his mother and Pat would be better off living close to Rafaela and Adela.

Victor was the first to arrive in San Antonio with all of the family's furniture and personal possessions. He rented a three-bedroom house near Rafaela, and Adela joined Victor, Pat, and their mother in the rented house. After paying the movers and the rent, Victor found that he had a five-dollar check in his possession which represented his entire financial resources. It was a personal check given to him by Alfred Egg for a full day's work putting in fence posts. The only problem was that no one in San Antonio would cash this out-of-town check for him. He was down to his pocket change after having ridden the bus in his attempt to cash the check.

He got off the bus in the vicinity of downtown on the near east side of the city. He had spotted the Southern Pacific Depot and he thought perhaps the ticket sellers might cash his check. He got in line behind several people he assumed were waiting in line to buy train tickets. A man in a gray suit came by and handed everyone in line, including Victor, a piece of white paper, and in a loud booming voice shouted, "Fill out this form and give it to the teller at the ticket window."

Victor looked at the piece of paper and realized that he had been standing in line with people seeking work with the Southern Pacific Railroad! "What luck," he thought as he quickly filled out the application. When he reached the teller at the ticket window Victor handed over the form and the teller looked at him, glanced at the piece of paper, and said, "Okay. Have a seat right over there with those men. We'll call you in for a physical exam when the doctor arrives."

Victor had never had a physical. The only time he had ever seen a doctor was when he was five years old and suffered a broken collarbone while playing tackle tag with children in the neighborhood. Dr. Wells had set his collarbone and made him wear a harness and a sling for three weeks. Even in college athletics he was never required to take a physical. Victor wondered what kind of a job this might be that required a physical exam. He looked around the room at the others waiting there, and he figured they were all in their mid-thirties or early forties.

There were about ten men including Victor, and one by one they were called in to see the doctor. When Victor heard his name, he went into the examination room and was told to remove all his clothes. The doctor took his pulse, listened to his heart, and checked for a hernia. He had Victor bend over and touch his toes, read a chart on the wall, and finally he asked him to provide a urine sample, handing him a small jar with Victor's name written on a piece of tape. Then he was told to get dressed and wait outside. When Victor returned to his seat, there were only four men still there — all that were left of the original ten applicants. They waited for another hour, then the man in the gray suit returned and handed each of them an envelope. He told them there were three meal tickets and a train pass in each of their envelopes. "You need to be here Sunday morning at 5:30 a.m. to catch the Sunset Limited train to Weimar, Texas," the man said. "You can use the train pass to take care of your transportation fare, and the three meal tickets can be used on the train or anywhere in Weimar. When you get to Weimar, see the ticket clerk there and he'll direct you to the work train where you'll be assigned."

144

Weimar was some 85 miles east of San Antonio, and Victor and the other four men arrived there about 8:00 a.m. The ticket clerk took them to the work train which was temporarily resting on a side rail just west of the small town. The train consisted of a coal-burning steam engine, a flatbed car that contained a crane and all of the equipment, two cars with bunk beds and showers, a dining car, and a caboose. The clerk told them they could sleep in any bunk bed that was not already taken. He said breakfast would be served at six and they should be ready to go to work by seven. "Mr. Cross will be your foreman and he'll meet you at breakfast time."

Victor woke early as usual that Monday morning. He put on the same work clothes he had used the previous summer while working for the Highway Department. Dressed in his tan khaki shirt and pants and wearing his army-type combat boots, he went to breakfast in the dining car with the other men. Victor was the youngest of the men since he was only twenty and most of the others were forty or older. He learned during the breakfast conversation that the permanent work crew consisted of seven, and that he and the other four were only temporary workers for the duration of the summer. The job of the railroad train crew would be to repair bridges and train trestles between Houston and San Antonio. After breakfast, Mr. Cross assigned them to some of the more experienced members of the permanent train crew and told them they were to serve as helpers.

Working for the Southern Pacific Railroad during June, July, and August under a hot Texas sun was an enlightening experience for Victor. Although their normal workday was eight hours, it was not unusual for the crew to have to put in a twelve-hour day. This was because the work was often dictated by the train schedules that were routed on a sometimes irregular basis, and the work to be completed was delayed.

It was hard, dirty, and often very dangerous work. Though the men were constantly reminded of certain safety regulations, accidents did occur along the route. In their second month, while working on a railroad

145

bridge on a hot humid day, one of the helpers fell to his death from the top of a thirty-foot bridge. It was never clear what actually caused him to fall, and speculation ran rampant in the minds of the men. Some said he had fainted after suffering a heat stroke. Others surmised that the man had a drinking problem. After hearing several versions of what happened, it came as no surprise to Victor that two of the fellows who had been hired with him quit at the end of the month. With one of the new-hires dead and two men quitting, that left only Victor and one other man to serve as helpers to the more experienced members of the permanent crew.

In the middle of August, a torrential rainfall washed out several of the bridges and railroad crossings. The train crew often found themselves working twelve and fourteen hours a day to repair or restore the washed-out bridges. The second week in August the last of the four men who had been hired with Victor left his job one night and was never heard from again. Now Victor was the sole helper for the members of the permanent train crew. Since he needed the money to help his mother, he never considered quitting. Besides, the members of the permanent crew had begun to consider him one of their own.

When August came to an end, Victor said goodbye to the members of the crew and thanked Mr. Cross, the foreman. He had worked hard that summer and had earned the respect of the hard-working members of the permanent train crew. Most importantly, he had learned to appreciate even more the importance of an education. While he admired and respected the men on the crew, some of whom had been with the railroad for twenty or more years, he couldn't see himself doing this kind of work as a career.

As he rode the Sunset Limited back to San Antonio, he could hardly wait to see his mother and sisters. And he now looked forward to entering North Texas State with greater interest and anticipation.

North Texas State

The fall semester at North Texas would begin in mid-September and Bill Walters had made arrangements to drive to San Antonio to pick Victor up. From Edna, the trip via San Antonio was only about 130 miles, but it was another 300 miles from San Antonio to North Texas State.

Bill got to Victor's house at mid-morning on Saturday. Manuela had packed them a lunch and after loading Victor's trunk in the car, the boys were on their way to Denton, home of North Texas State. The trip took about six and a half hours so they arrived around five thirty. At the athletic dorm they were assigned a room together.

Victor was excited about attending North Texas State — not just because he had never lived this far away from Edna but also because he was awed by the size of the enrollment and the expanse of the campus. In 1952 North Texas State was the fourth largest college in the state, with an enrollment of over 5,000 students. During registration, Victor saw that the student body seemed to be entirely Anglo-American. There were no Black students and if there were any others of Mexican-American origin, he didn't see them at that time. He was self-conscious as he went about the task of filling out his class cards and as he proceeded from one line to the next in search of the course numbers which were placed on the wall behind the instructors and student assistants seated at the tables. However, everyone was courteous, polite, and friendly to him and Victor was made to feel very special. He had never seen so many beautiful girls before and all of them seemed genuinely interested in returning his greetings or smile.

He enjoyed standing in line waiting to register for the various courses. It gave him an opportunity to carry on a friendly conversation with students all around him, Some asked where he was from. Others asked which dorm he was staying in. The girls in particular seemed to seek him out and he was flattered by all of this attention. After registration, Bill met Victor at the student union building and offered to take him to the athletic office to see Pop Noah, the track coach. As they entered the athletic office, Bill asked the receptionist if they could see the coach, but before she could answer, he appeared in the door to his office.

"Hello, Bill," Pop said in a friendly tone and then turned to Victor and said, "Hello, Fred." Pop had forgotten his name!

"My name is Victor," he corrected him as Bill watched with amusement. After chatting with Pop for a while, the phone rang and the receptionist told the coach he had a call.

"Let's go, Fred," Bill said with a mischievous grin on his face. It didn't take long for the word to circulate among members of the track team that Victor had assumed a new name. For the remainder of his three years at North Texas State, everyone on the team referred to Victor by his new name of "Fred."

Victor had enjoyed tremendous success as a half miler at Victoria College and had been widely recruited after winning the event at the National Junior College Championships in Kansas. But at North Texas he found himself running the mile and the half-mile races and finishing second behind his teammates Paul Patterson and Dale Imel. Paul had more speed than Victor and Victor could never beat him in the half mile. Dale had tremendous endurance and had only been

The two-mile relay team at North Texas State, 1954. Kneeling, Paul Patterson and Walter Abbey. Standing, Victor Rodriguez and Dale Imel.

148

defeated once in cross-country races. Victor could occasionally beat Dale in the mile run, but more often he finished a close second, but Victor could beat both Paul and Dale in running three laps (three-quarters of a mile). Thus, it was no surprise that North Texas was able to field a good two-mile relay team that was composed of Walter Abbey, Victor, Paul, and Dale.

During the years that Victor competed in track at North Texas State, there were only a handful of Mexican-Americans competing at the collegiate level. Ino Cantu, Victor's roommate at Victoria College, was an outstanding runner at the University of Texas in Austin. Joe Reyna was a Lone Star Conference champion at Southwest Texas State. And Javier Montes was an outstanding distance runner at Texas Western who became a member of the U.S. Olympic Team in 1952.

Victor's time at North Texas went by rapidly, and these proved to be some of the most memorable and rewarding years of his life. He would come home during the Christmas holidays to visit his mother and sisters in San Antonio, and in December of 1953 he managed to go to Beeville to visit Flo. She was even more beautiful than he had remembered, and he felt a renewed interest in continuing a relationship with her. They went to a movie in a downtown theater in Chencho Alaniz's car. Chencho was the husband of Lupita, formerly from Edna, whom Victor had known all his life and he was spending the night with them. Chencho had insisted that Victor use his car. After the movie, Victor took Flo home and said goodbye, and the next day he returned to San Antonio for the rest of the holidays.

Victor was one of only five Mexican-Americans at North Texas State. He stood out among the students not just as a rare Latino among a predominantly Anglo student body, but because of his personality which seemed to attract the friendship of other students, especially the girls. The boys would ask him to double date when their girlfriends' roommates were looking for dates. Arrangements with supposedly "blind dates" often turned out to be with girls who had already met Victor in the classroom or at some of the activities on campus.

*   *   *

In the spring of 1953, Victor was a member of the sprint-medley relay team which won the Drake Relays in Des Moines, Iowa. In the spring of 1954 he was a member of the two-mile relay team which won the Kansas Relays in Lawrence, Kansas.

Victor and Manuela had always been very close. When Victor was away from home, he was often challenged with decisions between the "harder right" or the "easier wrong." When faced with such a dilemma, he invariably felt the presence of his mother and her words of wisdom. He would recall her simple words such as "I know you will always do what's right" or "I'm proud of you." Or perhaps he would recall her parting words whenever he left the house by simply wishing him well with, "*Vaya con Dios.*" Then there were times in those student years when his financial resources were down to his last nickel, and on more than one such occasion, he would check his mailbox and find an envelope from his mother. There would be no message, but the two, three, four, or sometimes five dollars were self-explanatory, and Victor knew the tremendous sacrifice his mother must have made to send him the money when somehow she sensed that he needed it.

During June of 1954, Victor drove a tractor on a farm near Denton owned by R. L. Proffer. Mr. Proffer had hired him to work during the summer. He was busy during the day cleaning out the dairy barn and mending broken fences, and he drove the tractor in the evening until midnight because the tractor's engine would function better in the cooler temperatures after sunset. The tractor had headlights and it was a simple matter of keeping it on a straight course while the plows turned over the soil behind it. It was such a routine task that it sometimes bordered on boredom.

One evening when he was driving the tractor he was extremely tired. He had put in a full day helping Mr. Proffer bale hay and pick up and stack it. The evening was quiet except for the sound of the tractor's engine. About eleven o'clock Victor was about to doze off at the wheel when suddenly he heard his mother's voice. "Wake up, *mijo*," he heard her exclaim! He was so startled that he straightened up in the seat of the jerking tractor. He had almost gone to sleep! The thought frightened him because he could have fallen off the tractor and been cut to pieces under the sharp blades of the plows. He reached down and shut off the tractor's engine, picked up his water jug, and sprinkled water on his face. He sat there in the quiet darkness of the night fully aware of what had just happened. He was certain that he had heard his mother's voice.

All of a sudden he felt a strong need to see his mother. He left the tractor in the middle of the field he had been plowing and ran through the darkness to where the 1948 pickup truck belonging to Mr. Proffer was parked. He got in the pickup and drove into town to the Proffers' house. It was almost midnight as Victor knocked on the door. Soon the lights came on and Mrs. Proffer opened the door. She was surprised to see Victor standing there.

"Is Mr. Proffer here?" Victor asked.

"No, he had to go to Austin on a business trip," she said. "Can I help you?"

"No. I just need to go home for a few days and I wanted to let Mr. Proffer know. Please tell him that I'll call him in a couple of days."

With that, Victor went to his room in a boardinghouse, took a shower, and walked to the bus station to catch a bus to Edna. After an eight-hour ride, he walked to his sister's house. His mother had moved in with her daughter Theresa in Edna since falling ill a month earlier. His sister greeted him at the door, surprised and glad to see him standing there.

"I'm so glad you're here," she said. "I wanted to call you but I didn't know where to reach you."

"I was working on a farm this summer," explained Victor. "Where is Mom?"

"She's asleep now," Theresa said and told him that Manuela was ill and had been undergoing some tests at a hospital in Galveston and the preliminary diagnosis indicated cancer of the lungs. She also described the coincidence that the previous night just before Manuela went to bed she had expressed her desire to see him. Now as they talked, Manuela woke up. It was about 3 o'clock in the afternoon when she called out from her room, "Is that you Victor?"

Victor walked into her bedroom and was shocked to see her condition. She had lost a great deal of weight and her face was an ashen color. He sat on the edge of the bed and she reached up and touched his face with both hands. Victor bent over and kissed her on the forehead.

"*Mijo*, I'm so glad to see you!" Manuela said, trying to hide the pain that was possessing her. He sat there visiting with her until it was time for her medicine to control the pain. She soon fell asleep and Victor went to find a pay phone to call Mr. Proffer. When he finally reached him, Victor explained about his mother's illness and said he would be staying in Edna to help his sister take care of her.

So in that summer of 1954, just before his senior year in college, Manuela, Victor's mother, died of cancer at the age of fifty-eight. After he got back to North Texas in the fall, Victor had a phone call from Flo expressing her sympathy upon learning of the death of Manuela.

*   *   *

In the spring of 1955, Victor was honored by being named to "Who's Who Among Students in American Colleges and Universities." He graduated with a bachelors degree in art education.

U.S. Army –
The "Spearhead Division"

Victor didn't have long to ponder what to do after graduating from North Texas State. Rafaela and Frank Munoz, his sister and brother-in-law, attended his graduation ceremony and drove him back to San Antonio. He had thought about what he might do now that he was a college graduate. Along with his BA degree he had earned a teaching certificate, but he had never seriously considered teaching as a profession. At that time, teachers were earning a little over $2,400 a year and he wasn't interested in joining a profession which paid so poorly. He was thinking of going into the field of advertising and earning at least twice the annual salary of a teacher.

They arrived in San Antonio on Sunday afternoon, after spending the night in Denton. The next day, the postman delivered the mail around midmorning and Victor received an envelope with broad red letters stamped on the outside reading "Greetings from Uncle Sam." The "Korean Conflict" was in progress and Victor had just received a letter from his draft board in Bay City, Texas, informing him that his scholastic deferment had expired upon his graduation from North Texas State, and he was hereby notified that he had been drafted.

On July 26, 1955, Victor reported for duty and was sent to Fort Ord, California, for six weeks of boot camp. Then he was assigned to the Third Armored Division and sent to Fort Knox, Kentucky, in preparation for a thirteen-month assignment in Germany. The Third Armored Division was stationed in Gelanhausen, a small village about thirty miles from Frankfort. Because of his background as an athlete, Victor was assigned to Special Services and he spent the remainder of his military career taking care of the athletic facilities which consisted of a gymnasium, a football field, and a baseball diamond.

The Third Armored Division had won its nickname of "Spearhead Division" while leading American forces across Europe during World War II. The term came from General J. Lawton Collins who said, "You will spearhead the attack," when issuing orders to the division commander. Spearheaders have since then established a tradition of "firsts" — first Americans to enter Belgium, first to fire an artillery shell at German soil, first to break through the Siegfried Line, and first to capture a German city.

*   *   *

It had been raining for three days in Gelanhausen and the baseball diamond was well saturated. The team had won the home field advantage due to its won and loss record during the regular season, and they were to host the baseball team from Frankfort in the second round of the play-offs with a doubleheader game. A third game would be played in Frankfort if the doubleheader resulted in a split. The games were scheduled for Saturday afternoon beginning at one o'clock. It had rained Wednesday and Thursday, and although the clouds lifted and the sun had shown brightly by midmorning on Friday, the field was thoroughly soaked.

Lieutenant Ken Hall, Victor's supervisor, received word that the game might have to be played in Frankfort where it had only rained on Wednesday. Colonel Joe V. Langston, the battalion commander, didn't want to lose the home field advantage, and he ordered Lt. Hall to report to his office and to "bring that Rodriguez man with you." They reported promptly to Colonel Langston and listened as he expressed his concerns. Then the lieutenant asked if he could have a moment to talk to Victor who had stood silent during the entire conversation. They went outside and sat in the jeep to ponder the situation.

Lt. Hall was about to say something when suddenly a helicopter flew low over their jeep causing both of them to duck and hold on to their caps.

"That's it!" Victor shouted, pointing at the helicopter which had landed in the nearby parking lot.

"What's it?" asked a confused Lt. Hall.

"The helicopter! We need four helicopters to get the field ready for play by tomorrow!"

"*What?*"

Victor explained. The helicopters could swoop about four feet above the playing field, creating a lot of wind with their swirling blades. With the aid of the sun, he estimated that the field could be dried in half a day. It was noon, and Victor and the lieutenant drove to the motor pool and explained the plan to Major John Hughes. The major listened politely at first, then began to frown.

"There is one big problem with your plan," he said. "First, we have a short supply of fuel on hand. The price of gasoline on the German market has risen to ninety cents per gallon. How will you solve that problem?" Then he added, "But if you can get permission from Colonel Langston to use fuel for this plan of yours, I'll siphon gas from our trucks and jeeps that are inoperable at this time."

Victor and Lt. Hall went to see Colonel Langston, and after hearing their plan he enthusiastically picked up the telephone. "Major Hughes," he said with a grin, "I have an idea that may help you solve the fuel shortage. Why not siphon gas from the inoperable trucks and jeeps in the motor pool parking lot?" Putting down the phone, he turned to Victor and Lt. Hall and said, "Go dry that field."

The next day, the Third Armored Division won the doubleheader baseball game against Frankfort.

* * *

On June 29, 1957, Victor was honorably discharged from the Army at Fort Chaffee, Arkansas. While some men begrudged being drafted into service, Victor had enjoyed his almost two years with the Spearhead Third Armored Division. As Manuela had often said, *"No hay ningun mal que por bien no venga."*

Two Lucky Days

Upon his discharge from the army, Victor took the bus from Fort Chaffee to Denton, checked into the only hotel in town, and went shopping for some civilian clothes. He called the placement office at North Texas State and made an appointment for job interviews the following day. Next morning, a secretary at the placement office found his file and asked him a few questions to update it.

"This is your lucky day," she said with a pleasant smile. "A representative from Proctor and Gamble is here to interview applicants for positions with their firm. If you'll have a seat in the waiting room, he'll visit with you as soon as he finishes his present interview."

In the waiting room, Victor sat down in a chair facing the only other person there — a young woman in a pastel blue suit which complimented her blue eyes and blond hair. She smiled at him and got up from her chair to come sit next to him. Victor thought there was something familiar about her, but couldn't be sure.

"I'm Ann Crocker," she said as she offered to shake hands with Victor.

"I'm . . ." Victor began but before he could continue she interrupted and said, "I know who you are, you're Victor Rodriguez. You were on the track team here and . . ."

Victor didn't let her finish. "Of course! You were our football queen my senior year here at North Texas! Of course I remember you!" They both stood and hugged each other.

Ann was even more beautiful than he had remembered her during their years at school. She was from Big Spring, Texas, and she had a natural beauty enhanced by her warmth and friendliness.

"What are you doing here?" Victor asked.

"I'm here to see Dr. Cotteral, the head of the girl's physical education department," she said as she reached up to straighten his tie. "There," she said. "That's better. Now sit down and tell me all about yourself."

Victor told her about serving in the army for almost two years and how he was now in the process of interviewing for a job. She listened attentively and when he finished she said, "You were one of the nicest persons I knew when we were here at North Texas. Did you know that several of the girls in my dorm were crazy about you?"

Before either of them could say anything more, the secretary came in and said, "Ann, Dr. Cotteral will see you now."

They stood up and Victor extended his hands to hold both of hers. She gave him a peck on his cheek and said, "Good luck with your interview. I'm so glad I got to see you."

Before Victor could return the compliment the secretary interrupted them again and said, "Mr. Rawlings will see you now, Mr. Rodriguez."

As Victor entered the interview room, Rawlings came from behind a large desk.

"Come in, Mr. Rodriguez," he said as he gave Victor a strong handshake. "I'm Charles Rawlings and I am here representing the Proctor and Gamble Company from Cincinnati, Ohio." He explained that his company was interested in expanding the distribution of their soap and detergents into Mexico and he was interested in finding someone who could help them pave the way as a public relations representative.

"The starting salary is $5,500 a year plus benefits and all expenses paid. I have examined your personnel file here at North Texas and I'm impressed with your qualifications. As an athlete you have proved that you perform well in competition. That, plus the fact that you are bilingual, fluent in both English and Spanish, are strong assets in your favor." Victor was given time to ask questions as well as answer them, and finally

Rawlings stood up, shook hands, and handed Victor his business card.

"The job is yours if you are interested," he said. "If you decide to come with us, call me and let me know no later than the first of September."

After he had closed the door behind him Victor could hardly repress a shout of joy. "Wow! You've got the kind of job you wanted!" he almost shouted. Just two days a civilian and here was a great job offer.

As he started down the stairs outside of the administration building, he heard a once-familiar voice call him.

"Hey, Rod!" It was Pop Noah, his old coach. They shook hands and hugged each other. "What are you up to?" Pop asked. Before Victor could answer, Pop invited him to lunch so he could hear all about it. They hadn't seen each other in two years and both were genuinely interested in being brought up to date.

Later they walked out to Pop's car and drove to the athletic office. Settled behind his desk, the coach said, "Victor, this is your lucky day. Sit down here while I place a call to Dallas."

Pop picked up his phone and asked the operator to get him the superintendent's office with the Dallas Independent School District. After a brief conversation, he hung up and turned to Victor. "I was talking to Dr. White, the superintendent of schools down in Dallas. He called me yesterday to say he's looking for a track coach and assistant football coach in the high school where I coached before coming to North Texas. I just told him about you and he is interested in talking to you."

Victor thanked Pop for the recommendation and went back to his hotel room. He hadn't mentioned the job offer from Proctor and Gamble, but he liked Pop and didn't want to appear ungrateful, so he decided to go ahead and follow through and visit with this Mr. White.

Victor didn't realize that Dr. W. T. White was a living legend in Dallas and throughout the state. He was revered in educational circles and considered almost godlike, both feared and admired, by people in the district. In 1957, the schools in Dallas and in most of Texas were still ethnically segregated. The only school superintendent Victor had ever known was Bascom Hayes, whom his mother had admired, respected, and whose advice she followed. Hayes was a scholarly man, very professional and serious about education but also friendly, courteous, and polite with all elements of the Edna community, besides being accessible to everyone. Dr. White was a powerful individual as superintendent of schools in Dallas. Even the members of the board who had hired him didn't dare to meddle in his operation of the schools. He headed a large bureaucracy and was pretty well isolated by the layers of assistant superintendents and directors under his authority. Dr. White knew Pop Noah from his days as an outstanding high school coach in Dallas and now as a fine coach at North Texas; otherwise, he would never concern himself with the filling of a teaching or coaching vacancy. His secretary and the various layers of staff and assistants generally screened his calls and spared him from such minor matters.

The day after his visit with Pop, Victor checked out of his hotel in Denton and rode the bus to Dallas, only thirty miles away. Storing his luggage in a bus station locker, he took a cab to the administrative offices of the Dallas Independent School District and at the main office was greeted by an attractive young receptionist who asked the nature of his visit or business.

"I'm here to see Dr. W. T. White," Victor said, with all of the poise and confidence he could muster.

"May I ask what you would like to see him about?"

"I'm here to talk with him about a high school coaching position."

"Have you filled out an application through the personnel office?"

"No, I understood that he was interested in talking with me."

"Just a minute," the receptionist said as she reached for the phone and dialed a number. As Victor stood waiting, a security guard within hearing came over and stood near the receptionist's desk. Meantime, the assistant superintendent of personnel and the superintendent's administrative assistant had also been summoned by the receptionist, and they too came and stood by her desk. There seemed to be a tension in the air. "This gentleman says he is here to see Dr. White," the receptionist told them. The administrative assistant, the assistant superintendent for personnel services, and the security guard looked at each other and seemed to be either amused or bewildered at the news.

"Dr. White usually doesn't deal with personnel matters," the receptionist explained to Victor. About that time the door opened and a dignified, white-haired gentleman came out of the inner office and handed a list of names to the receptionist, saying, "If any of these people call, set up appointments for them next week."

"Yes, Dr. White," the receptionist said.

"Did you say Dr. White?" Victor asked.

The elderly gentleman turned and faced Victor.

"Yes, I'm Dr. White. Who are you?"

"I'm Victor Rodriguez," Victor stated, relieved to finally make contact with the man.

"Oh yes. Let's go in my office," said Dr. White, much to the amazement of the receptionist and the other staff members. They went into the office and Victor was told to have a seat.

"I understand you were one of Pop's boys at North Texas prior to your enlistment in the army," Dr. White began. "I'm looking for a minority with some track experience to fill a key position in one of our high schools — as a matter of fact, it is the school where Pop Noah coached when he was an employee of ours. The position calls for someone to serve as head track coach and as an assistant football coach. From what Pop has told me, you meet all of the qualifications the job calls for. Sooner or later, we're going to have to begin integrating our faculties in this district," Dr. White explained. "So when can you start?"

Victor said he had a few questions he would like to ask.

"Go ahead, fire away," said Dr. White, but he continued, "You will be the first Mexican-American assigned to a coaching position at this level. The salary will be five thousand dollars a year which includes both your teaching and coaching pay. You will be responsible to the principal of the high school, the athletic director, and the head football coach. So are you ready to go to work?" He seemed to be growing impatient.

"I'd like to have an opportunity to speak with the principal, the athletic director, and the head football coach," Victor replied.

"What about?" Dr. White asked.

"I'd just like to visit with them to see if we have similar educational philosophies or if . . ."

Victor was startled when Dr. White, now visibly irritated, stood up, pounded his fist on the desk, and in an angry voice shouted, "Damn it, do you want the job or don't you?"

Victor rose too and with all the calmness he could muster said, "I'm sorry I upset you. Thank you for your time and for the job offer," and he turned on his heel and walked out of Dr. White's office and closed the door behind him.

As he walked past the receptionist desk, she smiled and asked, "Are you going to be with us next year?"

"No," replied Victor. "I'm on my way to San Antonio to visit my sister and after that I'll be working for Proctor and Gamble."

Ohio vs. San Antonio

Victor was back in San Antonio on August 6, 1957. He hadn't seen three of his sisters since the day he was drafted almost two years ago. His oldest sister, Rafaela ("Fela") Munoz, was living in the Alamo City and Victor wanted to spend a couple of days with her and her family before going to Edna to visit Theresa. Adela was living in Memphis, Tennessee, with her husband who was a dentist, and the youngest of the girls, Pat, was still in Germany where her husband was an Air Force sergeant. In fact, Victor had visited Pat when he was stationed in Germany.

The bus arrived in San Antonio late in the afternoon and Victor took a taxi to his sister's address on the east side of town just behind Fort Sam Houston on Coleman Street. It was a small two-bedroom frame house next to a creek which flowed behind it. As Victor got out of the cab, Rafaela and her husband came out to greet him, followed by their two small sons, Frankie and David. After a fine family dinner, they continued to sit around the table exchanging family news and listening to Victor's experiences in the army.

"Did you kill anyone?" Frankie asked. David, the younger son, was more interested in hearing about Victor's experiences in sports. Rafaela was curious about what Victor planned to do now that he was a civilian again, and he told them about the job offer to work for Proctor and Gamble in Mexico as a public relations representative, and the Dallas job offer, though without mentioning the salaries.

"Gosh, we haven't seen you for almost two years and you'll be gone again," said Rafaela. "You have a degree and a teaching certificate and there is a shortage of teachers here . . . you could get a teaching job and stay here in San Antonio." Victor remembered his interview in Dallas with Dr. White and he didn't relish the thought of dealing with another school district superintendent.

The next morning after breakfast Fela brought in the morning paper and showed him a classified ad soliciting qualified teaching applicants. According to the ad, a beginning teacher could start at a salary of $3,000. Victor showed no real interest, but out of courtesy and — most important — out of respect for his oldest sister, he finally promised her that he would look into it. Rafaela could be very persistent when she wanted to be, and Victor found himself being driven that very afternoon to the central administrative offices of the San Antonio School District (SASD) by his sister and her husband.

They dropped him off in front of the district headquarters with instructions to "Call us when you finish and we'll come pick you up."

"That's okay, I'll just catch a bus or a cab." Victor went inside the building with the intention of merely going through the motions of applying for a teaching job.

In 1957, the San Antonio School District was by far the largest school system in the city with an enrollment of 75,000 students. The city was still in the process of building its expressways, and the business establishments were mostly located downtown within the 75 square miles of the school district boundaries. There were no shopping malls in the suburbs yet. The schools in San Antonio were still segregated. That is, the Black students were not permitted to attend the schools primarily attended by Anglos and Mexican-Americans.

Victor was greeted at the SASD central office by a mature lady who was serving as receptionist as well as information representative.

"I'm here about the newspaper ad for teachers," Victor told her.

"Fine. If you'll fill out this application, I'll make arrangements for you to be interviewed."

Victor filled out the application and brought it back to her desk. After looking it over carefully, she asked if he had a wallet-size picture that she could attach. He found a black and white photo in his wallet. "Is this okay?" he asked as he handed it to the receptionist.

"It'll do fine. I've already made arrangements for your interviews if you're ready."

The interviewing process involved four people who held administrative positions in the district. Each interview lasted about half an hour.

The first session was with a middle-aged man named Morgan Wheeler. He was the personnel director and he spent most of his thirty minutes providing Victor with information about the school district. "If you're hired, you'll earn three thousand dollars a year and you'll have to be under a probationary contract for the first two years," he explained. "There is a vacancy for a sixth grade teacher in a new school that is not quite finished. It's still under construction but will be finished in about thirty days." He asked if Victor had any questions, but since Victor's plans were to go to Ohio and work for Proctor and Gamble he said no.

The receptionist took him next to see Miss Inez Foster, the assistant superintendent for elementary schools. She was an elderly lady who Victor assumed was nearing retirement.

"I see from your transcript that you have an all-level certificate and that you can teach all grades," she began. "I'm looking for someone who can teach sixth grade in one of our newest schools. Do you think you could handle a self-contained sixth-grade teaching position?" she asked.

"Sure," replied Victor, thinking he probably wouldn't even be offered the job. Besides, in a couple of days, he would be leaving for Ohio. He sat there as this kind old lady continued to talk, but he only really concentrated on what she was saying when she asked him a direct question, which he would answer with a polite "yes ma'am," or "no ma'am."

"Do you have any questions?" she asked finally.

"No, ma'am."

Next he was taken to see Raymond Arnold, the assistant superintendent for secondary schools. Arnold spoke in a quiet, deliberate tone as he explained that there were six other candidates being considered for this position. "With the beginning of school only a few weeks away, we don't have many vacancies left," he said. "If it should turn out that you are selected to fill this vacancy, would you accept the position?"

Now he was being put on the spot. "I would consider the offer and could let you know in a day or two," he answered, reasoning that he could politely call them the next day and turn down the job, if indeed it was offered.

The final interview was with Claude Kellam, athletic director for the school district. "Come in and close the door," he said. Victor thought Kellam the most impressive of the four interviewers. He was a tall, slender man with white hair, dressed in a gray suit, his royal blue tie held in place by a tie clasp with a diamond in the center. "Sit down and take about five minutes to tell me about yourself," he said. Victor sensed that Kellam was a serious, no-nonsense kind of man. As he talked about himself he realized Kellam was studying him closely. Victor told him about being the first in his family to graduate from college, about his work experiences with the highway department, with the railroad, and his army service.

When he estimated that his five minutes were up he finished by saying, "That's about it."

Kellam was smoking a cigarette in a holder that made the cigarette stick out about six inches from his face. "You didn't mention anything about your participation in athletics," he said.

"Well . . ." Victor began, but Kellam interrupted him.

"I know a great deal about you already. I know that you ran the mile and half-mile and that you played football in high school. I also know that you won the National Junior College Championship in the half-mile before going to North Texas on a full athletic scholarship. You are one of

Pop's boys. Unfortunately we have filled all of our coaching vacancies but we do have this one position available which calls for a special kind of person to fill it. I assume that Miss Foster and Mr. Arnold have talked with you about this position?"

"Yes they have, but I understand there are several applicants being considered," Victor said.

"There are applicants and then there are applicants," Kellam said. "This is a very special sixth-grade class. We are in the process of completing the building of a school over on the west side of town to be named James Fenimore Cooper Junior High School. It will house students in grades seven, eight, and nine. But two of the elementary schools that feed students into Cooper, namely Ruiz and Barkley, have no more room for their sixth graders so we're sending the excess sixth graders over to Cooper. Do you have any other job offers to consider at this time?"

Victor sensed that it would be a mistake to lie to this man. "Yes sir, as a matter of fact, I have been offered a job with Proctor and Gamble in Ohio," he explained.

"That's a long distance from here to there," Mr. Kellam said. "I assume that job pays more than teaching," he added.

"It pays about two thousand dollars a year more," Victor said.

"Of course money is important," Kellam said, "but sometimes money isn't the most important thing. The kind of person we need for this sixth-grade position is someone who has a great sensitivity for working with about forty kids in a self-contained classroom. They are all Mexican-American, some with limited English-speaking ability, and some who cannot speak English at all. They are poor kids who come mostly from single mothers who live in public housing. It's a shame you already have a job offer that pays considerably more money because I think you could not only help these kids, but you could also serve as a role model for them."

Mr. Kellam rose from his chair, and said "Good luck with your job in

Ohio." And then as Victor thanked him he added, "If you happen to change your mind, call me first thing in the morning."

Victor took a taxi to Fela's house and found her and Frank waiting to hear all about the interview. After listening to his detailed description, Fela said, "From the way you describe that sixth grade class, it kind of reminds me of Miss Lindberg and the forty kids in the Mexican-American school in Edna."

Victor went to bed that night knowing that in the morning he would have to make a decision whether to go to Ohio or to stay in San Antonio. He said good night to Fela and Frank using his mother's words, "*Hasta mañana, con el favor de Dios.*"

PART III

SAN ANTONIO
1957—

Beginning a Career with SASD

After a good night's sleep, Victor had a hearty breakfast with Fela and Frank.

"Have you decided what you are going to do yet?" Fela asked.

"No, not really," Victor replied. "They told me at the central office that they were considering several other applicants for the job," he added.

The phone rang and Fela went to answer it. She came back with a look of excitement and an urgent tone in her voice as she told Victor that a Mr. Kellam was on the phone and wanted to speak to him. Victor went into the living room and picked up the phone. After a brief conversation he came back into the kitchen and sat down.

"Well?" Fela asked anxiously.

Victor smiled broadly and said, "You are looking at the teacher of a sixth-grade class at Cooper School."

"Really?" Fela asked excitedly.

"Great!" said Frank.

The fateful decision Victor made on that August day in 1957 would mark the beginning of a lifetime career with the San Antonio School District covering a span of thirty-six years.

* * *

Cooper Junior High School was not completed when its doors opened to welcome its first student body. The cafeteria, gymnasium, and vocational shops were not finished, the asphalt parking lot wasn't paved, and the student lockers were leaning up against the walls in the hallway waiting to be installed. The principal, Arthur Turbeville, was new in his position, as were Victor and most of the other teachers. There was no maximum pupil-to-teacher ratio and most teachers had thirty or more students assigned to them. Victor and Pauline Garcia were the only teachers for the two sixth-grade classes. They began the year with thirty-eight students apiece but by the middle of October each of them had forty-eight. Victor and Pauline were absorbing all of the excess students from the nearby Ruiz and Barkley Elementary Schools.

The students varied in their ability to speak and write English as well as in their age range. Since there was no direction or guidance from any source to help them manage and teach such a large number of children with varied ability ranges, they were left to survive by their own wits and means. Victor relied on his memory of the way Lucille Lindberg had taught in the Mexican-American School in Edna, and utilized many of her methods and strategies. He also benefited from Pauline's company and the exchange of ideas on their journey to and from work. Since Victor had a car and Pauline didn't, they had a car-pool arrangement. This arrangement lasted for the entire fall semester. In the spring, one of the Cooper coaches was transferred to a high school, and Claude Kellam called Principal Turbeville and told him he was assigning Victor to the coaching job at Cooper. With these additional responsibilities, Victor had to stay after school to coach basketball and track, so the car-pooling arrangement with Pauline was terminated and she made arrangements to ride with another teacher.

From time to time, Victor talked to Florinda on the phone. She was an elementary teacher in nearby Harlandale School District. He invited her to go with him to the Cooper faculty Christmas party and she accepted.

Later he realized one day that it had been a long time since he had talked to her. He finally called and after a brief chat Flo told him she was seeing someone on a steady basis and was no longer dating anyone else.

* * *

In the summer of 1958, Victor returned to North Texas and began work toward a master's degree in education. He returned to Cooper School in the fall, and he and Johnny Hausman, the other coach at Cooper, both had very successful football seasons. Victor coached the "B" team and Johnny the "A" team which won the city championship.

Then Victor was moved into the junior school as a teacher of English and driver's education. Pauline Garcia had moved to Corpus Christi, Paul Rode had replaced Victor as the sixth-grade teacher, and Stella Naranjo, one of Florinda's younger sisters, had replaced Pauline. It was during a coffee break with Stella that Victor learned Flo had married a young man from the eastern U.S., a pilot in the Air Force. Flo had met him while he was going through pilot training at one of the air bases in San Antonio. Victor received the news of Flo's marriage with mixed feelings, although he didn't fully understand why. He liked Flo, but he had never really pursued a serious relationship with her. Yet the thought of her marrying someone else left him with an unexplained emptiness.

"He's a lucky fellow," he told Stella in the best-natured voice he could muster.

* * *

The next summer Victor returned to North Texas to continue work on his master's degree, and he met Martha Ramirez, a student at Texas Woman's University. She was from Zapata, Texas, and was completing work on a degree in library science. They dated steadily that summer and in the fall Victor returned to his coaching position in San Antonio and Martha began teaching in Laredo. During the school year, they kept in touch and visits on weekends became almost routine. They were married in June of 1960 and Martha found a librarian position at Rhodes Junior

High School in San Antonio. Rhodes was close to Cooper School and the athletic teams of these two schools were bitter rivals.

Victor had intended to return to North Texas in the summer of 1961 to finish his master's degree but his plans were disrupted by a long distance call from Bill Easton. Bill had been the track coach at the University of Kansas when Victor was competing in track at Victoria and at North Texas State. He had tried to recruit Victor when he won the half-mile run at the National Junior College track meet in Kansas. Coach Easton had just been appointed by the Mexican Olympic Committee to coordinate and direct the Summer Olympic Games to be held in Mexico City in 1968. He was once again trying to recruit Victor.

This time, he needed someone with some track experience who was fluent in Spanish to serve as his assistant. He explained that they would report to Mexico City in June of 1961 and remain there until after the Olympics were over in the summer of 1968. Since Mexican-Americans with collegiate track experience were a rare commodity, Easton felt very fortunate to know Victor on a personal basis. He asked Victor to send him a resume so that he could present it to the U.S. State Department along with his personal recommendation. Victor did but two weeks later he received word directly from the State Department that due to the limited number of Mexican-Americans with collegiate track experience the State Department would like to send him to serve as a sports specialist and advisor to Guatemala, Costa Rica, and Panama. Once again, Coach Bill Easton had failed in his attempt to recruit Victor.

So Victor spent the summer of 1961 in Central America. His assignment was to share his knowledge of track and field with local sports organizations to help them prepare for the Summer Olympics in Mexico. He returned to Cooper Junior High School in the fall.

The next summer he finished his masters degree in education at North Texas and in the fall he was named head track coach and assistant football coach at Lanier High School. Lanier was located in the near west side of San Antonio. It had enjoyed tremendous success in basketball under Nemo Herrera, a legendary coach during the 1940s. But even after having won the state championship in basketball, Lanier was still regarded as a poor school and was tagged with the nickname of *"La Garra"* (the rag) by friends and foes alike. They had on rare occasions broken even in football but more often had losing seasons. The rivalry with Tech High School downtown had become an annual tradition known as the Chili Bowl because both schools had primarily Mexican-American students.

In track, Lanier's only current claim to fame was a state champion in the half-mile run. His name was Richard Menchaca and he had not only won the half-mile run at the state meet but had tied the time that had been established by James Outlaw twenty-five years earlier. While Victor was coaching at Cooper he followed Richard's performances with a keen eye. He watched as the young man became a prime recruit of colleges and universities throughout the nation, and Richard's decision to attend North Texas State was due largely to his personal acquaintance and relationship with Victor. Other than this star, Lanier was little known for its performances in track.

During the fall of 1962, Victor was in charge of the junior varsity football team. He coached some thirty to thirty-five football players by himself, but during the morning hours before school he began organizing a cross-country team and he managed to recruit six runners the first week of school. He was also teaching five classes in art and he took advantage of this assignment by making posters that invited participants for his cross-country team. By the end of the second week, he had fifteen runners participating in the early morning workouts with Victor himself leading them through the neighborhood.

Again he used his position as an art teacher to promote his cross-country team when he bought four dozen T-shirts and designed a large L with wings on each side. The L and the wings were printed on the front of the shirts at chest level. The white T-shirts with the royal blue winged L were very attractive and the symbol became known as the "Lanier Flying L." By the end of the fourth week, Victor had twenty-six runners in the early morning workouts. He and his runners were now jogging three to five miles on alternate days. In the meantime, he attended to his duties as coach of the junior varsity football team. He had good kids to work with but they were lacking in size and speed. They also lacked self-confidence and self-esteem and they had very limited knowledge of football. In fact, none of them had ever seen a live collegiate football game. Victor made arrangements at Trinity University to allow his junior varsity football team free admission to a game between Trinity and the University of Mississippi.

The Lanier junior varsity football team finished its season with five wins and two losses. After football season was over, many of the team members joined the cross-country team. The runners had participated in several intra-squad trial runs at a three-mile distance and Victor was pleased with their performance. Anthony Mendoza, a little five-foot four-inch runner, had steadily dominated all runners in the three-mile runs. He was a freshman who had developed and increased his stamina over the two-and-a-half months of early morning workouts. With football season over, Victor was able to also give his afternoons to the cross-country team, and with the late addition of the football players, it had grown to sixty-five runners.

The early morning workouts continued with distance runs, and the after-school workouts consisted of speed work and interval pacing. These two-a-day workouts proved to be very beneficial to the Lanier runners as they entered and won three practice meets against Burbank, Tech, and MacArthur high schools. In mid-December, they competed for the first time in the city cross-country championships at High Lions Park. The Highlands Owls, coached by Howard Johnston, had consistently won this event since its inception. Highlands High School had always had outstanding athletes and this year was no exception. But the Lanier Voks, proudly exhibiting their Flying L, gave them a real run for the city championship with Highlands winning by a score of just 52 to 53. (In cross-country, the low score wins.) Lanier was led by Anthony Mendoza, Juan Rivas, Richard Quiroz, Lawrence Sanchez, Richard Lopez, Rufino Lopez, and Juan Robledo.

The Lanier cross-country team had come within one point of tying for the championship and two points from winning it in their first try for the city title. Their efforts were not in vain, however, for in the spring of 1963 they gained recognition on the track with strong performances in the 440-yard dash, the 880-yard run, the mile run, and the mile relay. Little Anthony Mendoza advanced beyond the district meet to the regional and state track meets as a freshman. Juan Rivas advanced to the regional meet along with Richard Quiroz in the half-mile run, and the mile relay team qualified for the regional meet. All in all, the Lanier cross-country team and the track team had enjoyed a most successful debut in Victor's first year at Lanier in the 1962–1963 school year.

In the next three years the Lanier cross-country team won the city championship every year, beating not only the Highlands Owls but all the other San Antonio high schools as well. On December 6, 1965, Anthony Mendoza and Raymond Guzman led the Lanier Voks to overwhelming victories in the junior and senior divisions of the San Antonio College Invitational two-mile run at San Pedro Park. The high-flying Voks won six of the ten trophies in the meet.

Then two weeks later, the Voks showed their heels to all schools in San Antonio by winning the city championship in cross-country with a low score of 25 points. In the spring, the track team enjoyed tremendous success. Some of the outstanding times recorded by track team members were the mile relay of Richard Solis, Juan Rubledo, Richard Lopez, and Larry Sanchez with a time of 3:25 in 1963, and the mile relay of Rufino Lopez, Juan Rivas, Richard Lopez, and Richard Solis with a school and district record of 3:21.3. Ralph Solis established a school record in the 440-yard dash with a winning time of 49.2 at the Metro Invitational Meet. Juan Rivas won district in the 880-yard run with a time of 1:57.1. Anthony Mendoza won the district and regional championships in the one-mile race and qualified for state with a school record time of 4:21.3.

*   *   *

The success of the cross-country teams and the track teams of 1962 through 1966 school years have never been matched by other Lanier runners. They stand out in Victor's memory and are surpassed by only one other event, which occurred in the fall of 1965. His son, Rene James Rodriguez, was born on August 26, 1965.

From Lanier to Highlands

Victor was approached by Berry Ehlert, athletic director of the San Antonio School District, in the summer of 1966 to serve on a two-man team to develop a curriculum guide for physical education. The other member of the team was Howard Johnston, the track coach for Highlands High School.

Victor and Howard had been the pioneers in promoting cross-country in San Antonio before it was officially sanctioned and sponsored by the University Interscholastic League. They were fierce competitors in cross-country, with Lanier holding a 3-1 advantage as city champions over the past four years. Highlands had always dominated all San Antonio schools in track, but Lanier had fared well in the 440-yard dash, the 880-yard run, the mile, and the mile relay against Highlands. The two coaches not only respected and admired each other, but considered each other friends. Howard was the writer for the curriculum guide in physical education. Victor, because of his art teaching experience, was assigned the task of illustrating the guide. The two coaches worked hard all summer and were each paid five hundred dollars for their work.

In the middle of June, Howard was promoted to vice-principal at Highlands. This left a vacancy for a track coaching position there which was advertised statewide and drew applicants from throughout Texas, Louisiana, and New Mexico. Highlands had just won the state track championship the previous spring and the position of track coach at the school was considered a highly prestigious one. In fact, that spring Highlands had won every track meet they entered, beginning with the Border Olympics in Laredo and finishing with the 4A State

Championship in Austin.

June and July came and passed quickly, and Victor and Howard were nearing completion of the curriculum guide. Many people had been interviewed for the track coaching position at Highlands but no decision had been made. Meantime, Victor had been approached to become the running coach for the U.S. Modern Pentathlon Team which was to be permanently stationed at Fort Sam Houston in San Antonio. It would be a part-time position, since the day's schedule would have to be shared with coaches of pistol shooting, fencing, horsemanship, and swimming. After carefully considering the opening, Victor opted to remain a full-time art teacher, head track coach, and assistant football coach at Lanier. In the process of a discussion with the Pentathlon officials, Victor was asked if he could recommend someone else for the job, and he instantly recommended Howard Johnston. The following week, Howard was interviewed and officially appointed running coach of the U.S. Modern Pentathlon Team. Since he would be a vice-principal during the regular school day, he could schedule his running responsibilities after school. This position was tailor-made for him!

The second week of August, Victor and Howard presented the final draft of the physical education curriculum guide to Berry Ehlert and were complimented and thanked for a job well done. They were about to leave the office when Claude Kellam walked in. Kellam had been promoted to assistant superintendent for administrative services, and Ehlert's athletics department was one of many which fell under his umbrella of supervision.

"I hope I'm not interrupting anything serious, but I'd like to talk to Berry and Coach Rodriguez," Kellam said.

"You're not interrupting anything. We were just finished with our business," Ehlert replied.

Howard left and Kellam came in and closed the door behind him. "Berry, have you talked to Victor about our discussion this morning?" he asked.

180

"No, I haven't. I was just about to when you walked in."

"Why don't we both talk to him then," said Kellam as he sat down next to Victor in front of Ehlert's desk.

Kellam nodded to Ehlert who said, "Vic, I need a good track coach at Highlands High School. We've interviewed several good applicants but Claude and I both feel that you are the best man for the job. We were wondering why you didn't apply for it? You've done a great job at Lanier and you've established a fine program there, but Highlands just won the state championship in track and we need you to take over that program. You are the only coach who has beaten Highlands in cross-country and have competed well in track."

Victor thought for a moment and said, "I like the kids from Lanier and I'm very happy teaching and coaching there. This is my ninth year in coaching and now that I have completed my master's degree, I was seriously considering accepting a vice-principal position. I've already turned down two offers as vice-principal at the junior high level, but now that I have a son, I am more inclined to think seriously about accepting an administrative job. I didn't apply for the track coaching position at Highlands because I figured that if you were interested in me, you already know what I can do without an application. Besides, I am very happy at Lanier and I have some real good kids coming back next year."

Kellam and Ehlert were silent for a moment and then Claude Kellam spoke in a very deliberate tone as if to give emphasis to his remarks. "This district is bigger than any individual in it. Sometimes we have to make decisions at our level that are for the best interest of the district. Highlands won the state title and they are returning a good number of those kids this year, and we need to provide them with the best coach we can find. Berry and I are of the opinion that you are the right person for the job."

Victor said nothing so Kellam added, "I'm going to be very candid with you, Vic. The facts are that Highlands is a predominately Anglo school but we are beginning to have an influx of Black and Hispanic kids there. We need someone like you to be a role model for all the kids."

Victor was still silent as he considered their arguments, and then Berry Ehlert said, "You have an opportunity to be the first Hispanic to be assigned to a predominately Anglo school in San Antonio, but most important and foremost in making this decision, the fact is that you are the best qualified person for the job."

Kellam spoke again, "A year from now if you are still interested in an administrative job, I'll personally recommend you, but right now we need you at Highlands." And Victor finally acquiesced.

In the summer before assuming his duties as track coach at Highlands, Victor visited the homes of as many members of the Highlands track team as he could locate. He wanted to get to know his runners but he also wanted to know their parents. In the fall he was an assistant football coach in charge of the sophomore team of sixty-three players. They won five games and lost two. At the same time, he was working with the cross-country runners before school. Once football season ended, he concentrated all his time and energy on the cross-country team. Implementing the same program that had brought Lanier city championships for the past three years, Highlands won every cross-country meet that fall including a perfect ten-point score in winning the city title.

The Highlands track team began their season in the spring of 1967 with a victory at the prestigious Border Olympics in Laredo. They went undefeated the entire season prior to entering the state track meet. Highlights of the team's efforts were victories at the Invitational Metropolitan Track Meet and splitting the track team into two squads to win the Alamo Heights Track Meet and the Holy Cross Track Meet on the same day! At the State meet, Herb Ellison won the 220-yard dash, finished second in the 100-yard dash, and anchored the 440-yard relay to a second-place finish, and he was the high-point man at the meet. The

Highlands Track Team finished second behind Spring Branch of Houston.

*   *   *

The '66-'67 school year proved to be very successful in Victor's coaching career. One of his fondest memories and recollections was the half-time show during the Highlands–Edison football game in the fall of 1966. The Highlands Brigade (the cheering squad) dedicated the half-time performance to Victor and his family. The theme of the performance was "Thank Heaven for Little Girls," to celebrate the birth of Victor's daughter, Sandra Rodriguez, who was born on October 5, 1966.

From Vice Principal to Personnel Director

I n August of 1967, Victor received a phone call from A. W. Norton, the assistant superintendent for administration, telling him to contact Bill Mahan about interviewing for a vice principal position at Brackenridge High School. Mahan was the Brackenridge principal and he was looking for a replacement for Pat Shannon who had accepted a position as principal with the Harlandale School District, a suburban district just south of the San Antonio School District (SASD).

After a two-hour interview on a Sunday afternoon, Mahan decided to recommend Victor for the Brackenridge job. He and Victor got along well, sharing their backgrounds as coaches. Although Mahan was some fifteen years older, they also shared a good work ethic and both could relate well with people. Victor was put in charge of discipline, registration of new students, parent conferences, preparation of teacher schedules, maintenance of permanent record files for students, and of course would act in the absence of the principal. He remained in that job for two years. In 1968, Oscar Miller retired as superintendent, and the board of education hired Dr. Harold H. Hitt as his replacement. Claude Kellam was promoted to assistant superintendent for personnel services. Meantime, the U.S. Office of Civil Rights issued a directive to the SASD to integrate the faculties in all schools in accordance with the percentage of student ethnic population in the school district.

Prior to this time the Black teachers had been assigned to all-Black-student schools, the Hispanic teachers to predominately Hispanic-student schools, and the Anglo teachers to predominately non-minority schools. Kellam was placed in this position because of the tremendous reputation he had earned as a taskmaster in dealing with difficult problems. Dr. Hitt gave him a great deal of latitude in running the personnel office including a free hand in selecting a personnel director to assist him.

In June of 1969, Kellam promoted Victor to director of personnel. When he asked who he would be reporting to, Kellam said, "You will report directly to me on most occasions and to the superintendent if he deems it necessary. You'll be responsible for recruitment interviewing, hiring of teachers, and assisting the superintendent and me in assignment and reassignment of administrative personnel. You'll also be responsible for supervising the maintenance of all personnel files and records. Do you have any questions?"

Victor thought for a moment and then asked, "Yes sir, when do I start?"

"Yesterday," Kellam said, and added, ". . . but you will not *officially* start until the school board acts on my recommendation to the superintendent next Tuesday." The board unanimously approved the superintendent's recommendation and Victor became personnel director.

The work in the personnel office proved to be very difficult as they attacked the task of balancing and integrating the faculties in all schools. In the meantime, the expressways had dissected the district and displaced quite a number of people. These same expressways made the suburbs more accessible so that while the SASD was losing 1,000 to 1,500 students each year, the suburbs were growing by leaps and bounds. SASD found itself having to compete for teachers with these fast-growing suburban districts. Instead of waiting for vacancies to occur, Victor conducted a trend analysis of the previous three years to establish the average number of teachers they would need in the various grade levels or disciplines. Based on this analysis, principals were sent to colleges and universities to interview teaching candidates all over Texas and adjacent states. Kellam and Victor found themselves working fourteen- to sixteen-hour days during their first year together.

* * *

One day in the spring of 1970, after a full day interviewing teaching applicants, Victor received a surprise visit from his old high school classmate Pat Davis. Victor and Pat had not seen each other since their graduation night from Edna High School in 1951. Victor was fond of all his classmates, but he had special warmth for Pat and his efforts in preparing Victor for his final test in chemistry. They hugged each other as only friends who have not seen each other for nineteen years can hug.

Pat looked the same, still with that radiant smile, and he looked even more intelligent than he had in high school.

"What in the world brings you to San Antonio?" Victor asked.

"I'm looking for a teaching job in political science or government," Pat replied. "I've been teaching in California for several years and I want to come back to Texas."

Victor had no concern about Pat's teaching ability. After all, had he not been successful at mentoring and preparing Victor for his chemistry exam? But he also knew that Pat was a proud fellow and he wouldn't expect any special favors in the formal interviewing process.

"Fill out this application and give us about five days to process it and check out your references," Victor said. "I'll call you when we have received a copy of your transcript and teaching certificate."

After the formal interview was over, they spent a few more minutes chatting about common friends and acquaintances until interrupted by Victor's secretary telling him his next appointment was waiting. Victor and Pat shook hands and Pat said, "I'll look forward to hearing from you."

"You can count on it."

After a week had gone by, Victor called Pat to come for a second meeting. "Your application has been fully processed," he told him on arrival. "You have excellent credentials and references — which doesn't surprise me a bit — and we have a job for you at Sam Houston High School."

"Great," Pat said as he took the employment agreement to review and sign.

"You are now a teacher with the San Antonio School District and we are proud to have you with us," Victor said.

"Thanks. How about I buy you lunch?"

"No, I'll buy *your* lunch," Victor replied.

They drove to a nearby restaurant and after lunch Pat said, "Now that you have hired me, I want to share something with you about the chemistry test you took your senior year at Edna High School."

"Boy, I'll never forget that test! I really worried a lot about it, especially since everyone in Edna knew about my predicament. I was both shocked and pleasantly surprised to find out I made a grade of 95 on that test without looking at the chart on the wall."

Pat smiled broadly before breaking out into full, all-out laughter.

"What are you laughing about?" Victor asked.

"Now that it's all over, I think the whole incident about the chemistry test is funny," Pat said as he kept on chuckling. "I uncovered the wall chart with all of the elements and formulas in Mr. Ray's room before you took that test," he explained. "But when I told Babe McDowell about it he was absolutely certain that you wouldn't use it because you're too honest, so that night Babe and I broke into the chemistry room and found your test paper on top of Mr. Ray's desk. You made an 80 on the test but I changed about three more of your answers to make certain you would pass."

"Well, I'll be darned. That explains why Mr. Ray asked me if I had erased and changed some of my answers."

"After we had broken in, Babe got the idea about putting the three chickens in the hallway," Pat said. "So we went across the street and took three of George Simon's chickens and put them in the hall, figuring that way no one would suspect the real reason we broke in and they would think only of the three chickens left there by some pranksters."

Victor sat there amazed. After all these years the mystery of the erased answers had been explained! But he was personally satisfied to learn that he had made an 80 on the test without looking at the wall chart containing the chemistry elements.

*   *   *

As he drove home that night he reflected on this first year he had spent with the school district as personnel director. Nineteen-seventy had been good to him even though he had had to survive many long days and tough issues.

He had another reason to celebrate this year. On August 25, 1970, Carlos, his youngest son, was born.

The Pre-History of
an Effort to Change

Before September 1968, the San Antonio School District was in many respects a closed corporation, and as a result it dealt with the problems of education in a somewhat one-sided and narrow perspective. The district administrative offices were centrally located and administered by the superintendent and his staff. School board meetings were held at noon and the general public was little involved. This practice set the trend upon which most of the school principals based their own mode of operation in administering "their schools" and in dealing with the community. The principal in his own domain possessed the only answers to the social and educational problems of the teachers and students in his school. As long as the personnel in his school and the people in his community accepted his philosophy and thought and acted in accordance with his philosophy, he was convinced that he was doing a superb job. Very rigid dress and grooming codes were enforced in all schools. Course offerings were, of course, more adequate in some of the more affluent areas than they were in the economically deprived areas.

Many of the principals had held their positions in "their" schools for periods ranging from fifteen to twenty-five years. One of the remarks often made by a former superintendent was that sooner or later it was going to be necessary for the district to float a bond issue in order to buy the schools back from certain administrators.

A series of shock waves struck the school district in the fall of 1967.

People began accusing the schools of being closed to the community. It was indeed a traumatic experience when students in one of the high schools petitioned to secure changes in the curriculum and school policies which they felt adversely affected them as students.

The next year, the school board decided it was time for a change, but they didn't know what kind of change or exactly how to bring it about. The superintendent decided to retire, and the school board interviewed and screened more than twenty applicants for the job before making their selection. The majority of the applicants were people who already worked for the district, but the board decided they needed someone who had experienced success outside of SASD, and they found Dr. Harold H. Hitt, who had been very successful as superintendent of schools at Midland, Texas, for the past fifteen years.

Dr. Hitt reviewed the district's structure very carefully. He realized that SASD was too large to manage with a central administrative staff so he decided to decentralize. He divided the district into three areas, and each area administrative office was headed by a deputy superintendent and staffed with consultants for math, English, social studies, physical education, special education, practical arts, and guidance and counseling. Each area deputy superintendent was responsible for supervision of three high schools, six junior high schools, and twenty-two elementary schools. The central office staff was headed by the superintendent and his associate superintendent and four assistant superintendents. The duties of these assistant superintendents were broken down as follows:

1. The assistant superintendent for instruction and curriculum supervised a staff of three directors in the areas of curriculum, pupil personnel services, and federal and special programs.
2. The assistant superintendent for administration was responsible for school construction, pupil accounting, health services, the athletic program, transportation, and the ROTC program.
3. The assistant superintendent for business was in charge of

directors in the areas of payroll, finance, accounting, food services, purchasing, and plant maintenance.

4. The assistant superintendent for personnel services supervised directors of certified personnel and of classified personnel.

Victor was vice-principal at Brackenridge High School at the time of the decentralization of the school district. He was reassigned and promoted to director of certified personnel in March 1969. He was the first Mexican-American to hold an administrative position at this level.

From his new job, he was able to observe the operation of SASD in the three decentralized areas. Area I and Area II seemed to make the transition and establish their method of operation rather effectively in their communities although they had their difficulties from time to time. Area III was in a constant turmoil during the next two years. There were two student walkouts in secondary schools. Some principals were insecure and very defensive in their approach to community involvement. People in the community were accusing some of the principals of discrimination and demanding that they be fired. The Area III high schools didn't provide some of the course offerings that other high schools were providing. Teachers were somewhat reluctant to go out into the neighborhood. The community was demanding that the deputy superintendent be replaced with someone more sensitive to their problems and needs.

In July 1971, Victor was called into the superintendent's office and advised that he was being promoted and reassigned to Area III as deputy superintendent. He asked for a few days to consider the promotion before officially accepting it. The request was granted, and for the next two days Victor did some serious thinking and soul-searching.

He had begun his teaching career as an elementary teacher in Area III. He had spent ten years as a coach and teacher in two of the "tough" junior and senior high schools in that area and was generally successful

in both schools. He had also taught and coached in one of the more affluent schools in another area before returning to Area III as vice-principal
of Brackenridge where he stayed for two years before becoming personnel director for the school district. Now he was being asked to return to
Area III as deputy superintendent.

Certainly he knew the Area III community and its schools very well.
It was a predominately Mexican-American community and in San
Antonio it is known as the "Westside." All of the schools there qualified
as Title I under the Federal government's criteria of identifying schools
for underprivileged or economically-deprived children. But the vast
majority of the teachers in Area III were Anglos. They lived in the more
affluent areas outside Area III and commuted to their jobs.

The people of the Area III community are good people. Most of the
parents of the students who attend the schools there have very little if any
formal education, and in the past, the community depended heavily on
the schools for the education of their children since they did not have
personal knowledge of how the system worked. Recently, however, they
had been influenced by several organizations, some of which were feder-
ally funded. These groups had taken it upon themselves to champion the
cause of the underprivileged or the economically deprived and made it
their responsibility to inform the community of their legal rights. Many
of these groups considered themselves the advocates of the people, while
others stayed well behind the scenes but nevertheless advised or coached
certain citizens to take the lead in questioning or making allegations
about schools or school officials.

Victor accepted the job as deputy superintendent because he felt that
he knew the problem from both sides. He knew that as long as he was
educationally sound in his approach to the community and to the school
district personnel he could at least get a hearing from both sides. He
knew the superintendent well and he had always respected his sense of
fairness and respect for the truth.

*   *   *

During July and August, Victor talked to many people who worked or lived in the communities within the boundaries of Area III. He was amazed at the lack of communication between the schools and the community and its many organizations. He was even more amazed, however, at the lack of communication within the confines of a single school structure. It was at this point that he decided if he was going to deal successfully with the turmoil and unrest in Area III, he was going to have to bring about better communication among the individuals within a school as well as between the schools and the community. He felt that if communications could be improved, then he could address the number one priority — the improvement of instruction.

He knew that he would have to directly or indirectly involve principals, consultants, teachers, students, parents, and representatives from the various organizations. And he felt strongly that if he were going to hold the principals responsible for providing the educational leadership for their schools and their communities, he would have to make certain that they clearly understood their role and their responsibility as an integral part of the overall structure.

During his two years as personnel director Victor had become well acquainted with all of the principals in Area III. He knew some of their strengths and some of their individual weaknesses. He met each one of the thirty-one principals individually during August before the opening of their schools. He discussed with each of them their administrative philosophy. He also solicited their opinions and allowed ample opportunity for them to express their feelings.

Next, he called a group meeting of all of them. They again discussed their goals and objectives and he received overwhelmingly positive reaction from most of them, but it was quite apparent that the principals did not have a good understanding of the structure of the school district, nor were they really aware of their individual roles as a vital part of the over-all structure. They had previously had little opportunity to discuss common problems among themselves and they welcomed the opportunity to interact in a principals' meeting. They were anxious to contribute, but wanted some assurance that they would be backed for assuming some initiative in community involvement. It was also obvious that little time had been spent in providing them with some kind of inservice concerning the role of the principal, promotion of staff morale, and the importance of good public relations.

The Substance of the
Effort of Change

When Superintendent Hitt decentralized the school district, he did so with the following goals and objectives in mind:

1. To provide better administration and supervision to improve instruction;

2. To establish administrative offices in each area to facilitate communication with school administrators, teachers, students, and parents; and

3. To deal with problems peculiar to the respective area or community concerning educational needs.

The principals agreed to involve their teachers and students and parents in open discussions of problems in their schools and their communities. They also agreed to involve the PTA and other neighborhood organizations in discussions which might improve school and community relations.

During individual conferences with the principals, Victor learned that no clear-cut goals or objectives had been established for the Area III schools. He held another meeting with the principals and devoted most of the time to reviewing the overall district structure. He explained to them that the main reason for the decentralization of the school district was to provide better administration and supervision in order to improve instruction.

While the principals were interested in improving instruction in their schools they were concerned about the immediate problem of doing something to calm the turmoil and unrest in Area III. They established an administrative advisory committee and Victor met with them regularly. He listened carefully to their suggestions and recommendations. They were worried about some of the unfavorable publicity their area had received in the press, and they were especially concerned about two of the schools which were under careful surveillance of the "militant" element. They decided that time should be spent in discussion groups in which all principals would be involved.

The thirty-one principals were divided into three committees:

1. Qualifications of a principal;
2. Promotion of staff morale; and
3. Public relations.

They were enthusiastic about their individual committee participation and there was much discussion and interaction on these topics. These might not have been as important at any other time, but now they served the purpose of involving the principals in discussion of common problems. They in turn carried the process a step or two further and appointed a committee of students, parents, and teachers to discuss problems of their own immediate school and community.

The rationale for employing this method of discussion was to specifically involve the principals. The administrative advisory committee felt that this approach would create a self-awareness on their part, because improvement of instruction was going to require a lot of work from them as the educational leaders of the school in promoting good staff morale and good public relations.

It was becoming more and more apparent that resistance to change was not the real problem. The real problem was a lack of communication between the very individuals who were the most directly involved, concerned, and affected by the effort of change. It was this same lack of communication that permitted allegations, rumors, and half-truths to develop and spread to unbelievable proportions. Victor was very much aware that understanding and communication would not be achieved instantly . . . nor could be achieved at all without overcoming many obstacles.

In initiating the first meeting, Victor failed to recognize the fact that many of the Mexican-American parents could neither read nor write English, but he soon resolved this problem by sending out invitations in both English and Spanish. The fact that the invitations were written in Spanish helped reassure some parents that his efforts at increasing communication channels were sincere.

Some of the open meetings were subjected to attempts by a few to further their own private campaign of promoting racial tension. The citizens involved took care of this situation by passing a resolution to prohibit discussions not directly concerned with educational problems or issues.

Some pressure was brought by parents upon the principals to retain the rigid dress and grooming codes. They didn't want their children to attend a school where they would be allowed to look like hippies. In some cases, the parents who were the most stubborn supporters of a strict dress code had sons and daughters who were the student leaders demanding the dress code be changed. To answer this problem, the school board set a policy that each school would handle their own dress and grooming code, and the principals allowed their student body to be involved in determining these policies.

A few principals were not prepared to be questioned by members of the community. Some had to learn not to be defensive in answering questions in open meetings, and some never did accept the fact that anyone would dare question them or their position. This situation was resolved to a degree by their voluntary resignation or retirement.

Some parents were reluctant to attend night meetings in a central meeting place, so the superintendent and the school board agreed to rotate the second meeting of each month among the different decentralized areas in order to involve the communities of the various schools. The administrators and teachers had to realize that it was not enough to meet the parents halfway. Rather, they must take the initiative in welcoming and reassuring the patrons.

* * *

Victor met with the presidents of the PTA's of each of the thirty-one schools in Area III and asked them to recommend fifteen people who might serve on the Area III Citizens' Liaison Committee, and to select those who would represent a cross-section of Area III. The purpose was to give representation to the individual community problems and to provide an open meeting where citizens could air their grievances or complaints.

At first, meetings of the Citizens' Liaison Committee took place in the Area III administrative office conference room. All fifteen members of the committee were present at the initial meeting, along with all the principals from the Area III schools. This was very successful, and by mutual consent of principals and citizens it was agreed that in the future the meetings would be rotated among the schools. The principals were very receptive to the suggestions made by the Citizens' Liaison Committee, and as a result of the joint communication the following results were accomplished:

1. Liaison committees composed of citizens of all ethnic backgrounds were appointed to serve in each of the three decentralized areas as a sounding board and a source of guidance to the school board, the superintendent of schools, and the deputy superintendents.

2. School board meetings were held each month in the various areas of the district to give patrons a better opportunity to see the manner in which the board functioned and to provide them an opportunity to express their opinions.

3. A committee of teachers, students, and parents was appointed to work with the administration of each school in designing and planning programs that would meet the specified needs of the students in that particular school.

4. A curriculum committee was formed for each discipline, composed of teachers appointed by the teachers' council, administrators appointed by the administrators' and supervisors' organization, and parents recommended by the PTA and appointed by the school board to study curriculum.

5. A policy committee made up of teachers and administrators was appointed by their respective organizations to recommend revisions in the school district policy book to the superintendent and to the school board.

6. Ad hoc committees of administrators were appointed to serve as reactors to virtually every proposed change in operational procedures.

7. Parents were utilized as tutors of students in their schools.

8. High school students were utilized as tutors in the elementary and middle schools.

9. College students were utilized as tutors at all levels.

10. Rigid dress and grooming codes became more relaxed.

Victor remembers the administrators who came to him as they planned to open the schools to the community. Some were enthusiastic, while others told him that as soon as they let those parents get their foot in the door they would "take over the joint." Fortunately, the bad omens did not become a reality.

Instead, the search for involvement has brought the resources of the entire community together in working towards the number one priority — the improvement of instruction in the schools. Today when they speak of the school community in Area III, they are referring to pupils, parents, teachers, administrators, and others.

* * *

In trying to promote better communication between the school and the community, Victor learned some valuable lessons about effecting change. Although he had been thoroughly familiar with the schools and the community of Area III as an elementary teacher, coach, assistant principal, and personnel director before becoming deputy superintendent, he found that these very experiences and associations sometimes made it difficult for him to deal realistically or objectively with the different situations. He often caught himself rationalizing or presuming that everyone wanted to accomplish the same goals he had in mind, whereas he found that most people were totally unaware of the overall structure of the school system. They were interested in it primarily from the point of view of their personal involvement or experience. He started out to revolutionize Area III by improving the curriculum and instruction. Instead, he became mired in trying to improve school and community relations before he could do anything about improving instruction. He had always considered himself a rather successful teacher and coach in Area III. When he returned to Area III as deputy superintendent, his new title created a barrier in working with some of the people. He often wished that he could have drawn the pay without that title. Some of the people who had been sincere with him while he was a teacher now communicated with him in accordance with what they felt he wanted to hear. They kept feeling him out.

In the final analysis, in his effort to effect a change, he himself became the biggest benefactor of that effort. He believes that this effort has made him more objective in dealing realistically with problem-solving human behavior. It made him realize that there are some things that he by himself could not change.

Victor is especially indebted to Dr. Harold H. Hitt for his fine leadership and to Mr. David Rusmisel and Dr. S. T. Scott for sharing with him their friendship and encouragement in some very critical situations as he performed his duties as deputy superintendent.

Promotions and Awards

During the 1973–74 school year, Victor was one of ten people selected nationally to participate in the Mid-Career Program in City School Administration at Yale University. This generous fellowship grant to study management and organization of large school systems even permitted him to take along his wife and children for the term of the study.

As a program participant, Victor took part in graduate level seminars and was a guest lecturer to students at the master's degree level. While studying the New York Public School System, he met Mario Fontini and Marilyn Gittel, professors at Columbia University. They were the authors of the voucher system that was introduced in New York in 1973 — a program that failed due to the lack of provision for transportation for the most needy students.

Victor returned to San Antonio in the fall of 1974 and Dr. Hitt promoted him to assistant superintendent for administrative services. He was assigned responsibility for the administration and supervision of plant services, food services, security services, publications, data processing, athletics, and health services. He was also responsible for coordinating the work of other assistant superintendents, maintaining the policy manual, and serving as the school district's liaison with city, state, and federal governments. He was in charge of the district in the absence of the superintendent which sometimes meant representing the district in board meetings. Victor served in this position for five years which provided him with an in-depth understanding of the inner-city school system.

In 1979, he was once again honored by receiving a fellowship as one of ten fellows in the Cooperative Superintendent's Program sponsored jointly by the University of Texas and the Texas Education Agency. While participating in this prestigious program, he helped the Texas Education Agency implement the Coordinated Monitoring System for all Texas school districts. In the spring of 1981, he was among the top three students in the doctoral program at the University of Texas at Austin and completed his Ph.D. in August of that year.

In 1981 Victor was appointed superintendent-elect to succeed Dr. Hitt who was retiring at the end of the school year. It was also the year that Victor became a single parent as the result of a broken marriage.

In the fall of 1982, Victor was appointed superintendent of schools and became the first Hispanic to attain this position in SASD. At that time the district was the fourth largest in Texas. He was also the first Hispanic superintendent among the twelve largest school systems in the state.

In the meantime, Flo had returned to San Antonio and, like Victor, she too was a single parent. During the next six years, Flo and Victor renewed their friendship and she became his constant companion in attending school-related functions and sporting events. They married on November 18, 1988.

Express-News

SAN ANTONIO, TEXAS   Thursday, November 24, 1988

● ● ●

The things teachers do when the students aren't looking . . . SAN ANTONIO SCHOOL DISTRICT Superintendent VICTOR RODRI-GUEZ got married last Friday to ROGERS ELEMENTARY SCHOOL teacher FLO HUTCHINS in ceremonies in CIBOLO . . . the groom's oldest son and the bride's oldest daughter served as witnesses in the private ceremony . . . .

During his twelve-year tenure as superintendent, Victor contributed to the following district accomplishments:

- The dropout rate was reduced from 50% to less than 10%.
- The teachers and other school district employees had the best salary and benefit package in Bexar County.
- In 1986, the school district air-conditioned all the schools to improve the teaching and learning climate. Previously, only 11 of the 95 schools in the district were air-conditioned.
- In 1981, as superintendent-elect, he had promised the kindergarten class that he would "stay in school" with them through their senior year. They were seniors in the spring of 1994, the year he retired as superintendent.

Victor was recognized statewide and nationally as a champion of children and gained many notable awards. The following represent some of them:

- 1985 - Achiever Award from the Alamo Area Council of Boy Scouts of America.
- 1986 - Award of Honor from the National School Public Relations Association for exemplary practice of good public relations in support of education both on and off the job.
- 1987 - Finalist in Texas Superintendent of the Year Award Program conducted by the Texas Association of School Boards.
- 1989 - Representative from Texas in the 1989 National Superintendent of the Year Award Program sponsored by the American Association of School Administrators and the Service-Master Company.
- 1990 - One Hundred Top School Executives in the Nation as selected by the Executive Educator Magazine, published by the National School Boards Association.
- 1990 - Presidential Citation for Outstanding Alumnus from the

University of North Texas.

• 1990 - One of five most outstanding graduates of the Department of Educational Administration, the University of Texas at Austin.

• 1991 - Honoree in Ford Motor Company's Hispanic Salute recognizing San Antonio Hispanics for outstanding contributions to education and the literacy effort.

• 1993 - One Hundred Top School Executives in the Nation as selected by the Executive Educator Magazine (as also in 1990).

Victor retired from the San Antonio Independent School District in 1994 at the age of 62. Since then he has been a consultant to the Texas Education Agency in dealing with troubled school districts and with Harold Webb and Associates on national school superintendent job searches. He has also served as a consultant to the Southside Independent School District, and the school districts of El Paso, Canutillo, Waco, Fort Worth, and Dallas, and as interim superintendent for four months in La Pryor and four months in Edna.

While serving as interim superintendent with the Edna School District in the spring of 2000, he recommended to the school board that the junior high school be named Meadie Pumphrey Junior High. The board unanimously approved the recommendation and Miss Meadie died only a few months later.

* * *

Victor and Flo enjoyed watching high school athletic events, and during the second week in November 1993 they were in Alamo Stadium to watch the traditional game between Edison and Jefferson high schools. This game drew special interest not only because it was the last game of the regular season, but also because this year both schools had earned the right to advance into the bi-district playoffs the next week. Edison would play Clark in Division II 5A and Jefferson would play in a Division I 5A game against Holmes.

There was a good crowd with enthusiastic supporters wearing their school colors. In recent weeks there had been several incidents in the communities of both schools involving fights between neighborhood gangs. The game itself was preceded by the normal pre-game activities including the school songs, the national anthem, and a moment of prayer.

The first three quarters were played with no sign of serious friction between the two teams except the penalties which occur in a normal game. Edison was dominating the game by 21- 0 with about two minutes left in the final quarter when suddenly players from both schools cleared their benches as they rushed onto the field and took part in an all-out brawl which caused the officials to call off the game. The spectators stood there in complete shock and disbelief. Security police, game officials, and coaches were successful in stopping the brawl and escorted the players to their respective buses.

Having served as chairman of the executive committee of the University Interscholastic League legislative committee, Victor knew the procedure that had to take place after such an incident as this. The strength of the UIL rests with enforcement of the state rules by the local executive committee of the UIL district in which the member schools participate. Victor summoned the school district athletic director and told him to convene the District 27 5A executive committee the following morning to discuss and render a decision regarding the misconduct of both teams. This committee was composed of the eight high school principals from Brackenridge, Burbank, Edison, Highlands, Jefferson, Lanier, Tech, and Sam Houston.

The principals met and after much discussion recommended a private reprimand and placing both schools on probation for one year. The probationary period would not begin until the next school year, thus allowing Edison and Jefferson to continue into their playoffs this year. The committee delivered their decision to Victor, but in the meantime the incident of the brawl was shown locally by the television channels. It was also picked up by national television stations which showed it with other examples of violence by athletes at collegiate and professional levels. Victor got a copy of the videotape of the brawl from one of the local stations and reviewed it several times to determine the degree of involvement by the participating members of each team.

He came to the conclusion that both teams were equally involved in the brawl and carefully considered his options and the possible consequences of any decision he might make. He took into account the following factors:

1. The two teams had qualified to advance to the bi-district state playoffs against Clark and Holmes the following week. Any departure from the decision made by the District 27 5A committee would have to be made immediately in order that the UIL in Austin could notify the Clark and Holmes teams of the decision.

2. He did not want to involve his school board, in the event he might decide to overturn the decision of the local 27 5A committee, and he was concerned about turning the issue into a political turmoil. He knew from past experiences that the school board would be subject to heavy lobbying from many sides. Besides, the board could not be involved in a special meeting without the posting of an agenda seventy-two hours prior to the meeting. This was clearly in keeping with the open meetings act requirement. This, then, would delay the notification of the UIL in Austin who in turn would be delayed in notifying Clark and Holmes High Schools.

3. Just the previous month Victor had announced to his board that he would be retiring at the end of December 1993. If he were to accept the decision of the District 27 5A committee of a one-year probation and a private reprimand, the probationary punishment

would take place next year. He would be retired and the punishment would affect next year's players and students while this year's seniors would get off scot-free and be permitted to advance into the playoffs with no consequences for their unsportsmanlike behavior!
4. Victor had served as state chairman of the UIL legislative council in past years and he was fully aware of how the League functioned when reports or appeals reached that level. There would be no guarantee that the UIL in Austin would accept the local decision made by the District 27 5A committee. It could overrule the local committee and issue a more severe penalty affecting next year's athletes and student bodies.

Victor had always held fast to a personal philosophy: "Schools should not be places where deficiencies are created . . . on the contrary, schools should be places where deficiencies are corrected."

Thinking over all these elements, Victor knew that he had to accept the responsibility of overturning the decision of the local District 27 5A committee. After all, he reasoned, all of the eight high schools of District 27 5A were schools in the San Antonio School District. He decided that it should be *this* year's athletes of both schools that should receive the punishment instead of next year's teams. He notified the athletic director and the principals of both schools that he was disqualifying both teams from advancing to the bi-district playoffs. He personally picked up the phone and notified Dr. Bailey Marshall, the executive director of the UIL in Austin, of his decision. Dr. Marshall explained to Victor that this was the first time in the history of the UIL that a superintendent had overruled his own local district level committee but he said he would notify the Clark and Holmes school officials of the decision.

There was instant state and nationwide attention to this outcome, and of course there was also a storm of protest from athletes and students from both schools, along with some of their parents. Legal machinations were attempted, fortunately to no avail. There were demonstrations protesting the superintendent's decision. Some of the players on both football teams as well as some students called the action unfair and unjust. Montel Williams, national television personality, contacted the SASD public relations office and invited Dr. Victor Rodriguez to appear on his talk show. Victor didn't want to glorify an already overly-publicized incident involving violence on the part of athletes, so he declined the invitation.

When Victor made his decision to disqualify both schools, he did so with the full understanding that he alone would have to accept the responsibility for his actions. During the days following his decision he was pleasantly surprised and completely overwhelmed by the positive support he received from sportswriters, newspaper editorials, teachers and school boards locally and statewide, churches, and people from the local community, as well as throughout the state and the nation. His office and the district PR office were bombarded with hundreds of calls supporting the decision.

The following week, at their regularly scheduled meeting, the members of the Board voted to reaffirm the superintendent's decision.

A Touch of Nostalgia

On the day of the 49th reunion of the class of 1951, as Victor and Flo took a tour of Edna, he was remembering the axiom that you can never truly go back home again, and he recognized the truth in that statement. On the route he once ran to ring the church bell, all of the sandy-loam streets had been paved. Not one single dog roamed free – they were either tied up or penned in their yards behind fences. The old St. Agnes Church was gone and in its place was a modern, air-conditioned structure with a new bell tower. The bell Victor had rung each morning was now rung automatically by an electrically-controlled device. Finally, Victor drove to the site where the old Mexican-American school had once stood. The school was gone – there was no trace of it left now. The site was covered by tall grass, underbrush, and large trees.

Victor stopped the car on the raised surface which had been the road to the old Mexican-American school. He got out of the car and stood there surveying the once familiar school site, and he could still see the young Mexican-Americans as they ran and played in that playground. He could recall many of their happy faces and their voices and laughter. He also remembered the remarks of Lucille Lindberg as she began every school day by reminding them that, "This is America, and if you work hard and are willing to compete, you can be anything you want to be." Only he and Chris Rosa had continued their education beyond the fourth grade and had managed to graduate with the class of 1951.

As he stood there overcome by nostalgia, recalling fond memories of the Mexican-American school, he thought of one particular memory that he would cherish forever. He remembered standing before his class attempting to master the art of recitation with the assistance and encouragement of his teacher. He was amazed that he could still recall the words as he slowly began to recite the poem:

The Fear of God
by Robert Frost

If you should rise from Nowhere up to Somewhere,
From being No one up to being Someone,
Be sure to keep repeating to yourself
You owe it to an arbitrary god
Whose mercy to you rather than to others
Won't bear too critical examination.
Stay unassuming. If for lack of license
To wear the uniform of who you are,
You should be tempted to make up for it
In a subordinating look or tone,
Beware of coming too much to the surface
And using for apparel what was meant
To be the curtain of the inmost soul.

Lucille Lindberg had handpicked him when he was in the third grade to perform his personal civic responsibility as the bell ringer for the St. Agnes Catholic Church. Why did she pick *him*? Why not someone else? Had she selected someone else he would not have benefited from the many lessons learned as a bell ringer. Perhaps it was an arbitrary god who influenced her decision.

Victor stood there for a moment with a feeling of enlightenment. Maybe it was the visit to the old Mexican-American school site that had enhanced his memory, or perhaps it had provided him with a more thorough understanding of the message in Robert Frost's poem. Victor got back in the car, and he and Flo began their short drive to the 49th reunion of the class of 1951.

Victor and Flo

CPSIA information can be obtained
at www.ICGtesting.com
Printed in the USA
LVHW111449180919
631476LV00005B/50/P

9 780934 955638